CHRIS SMITH

THE DIABETIC CHEF®'S
YEAR-ROUND
COOKBOOK

A Fresh Approach to Using Seasonal Ingredients

American
Diabetes
Association®

Cure • Care • Commitment®

Director, Book Publishing, Robert Anthony; *Managing Editor, Book Publishing*, Abe Ogden; *Editor*, Greg Guthrie; *Production Manager*, Melissa Sprott; *Composition*, ADA; *Cover Design*, pixiedesign, llc; *Cover Photography*, Cade Martin; *Printer*, Transcontinental Printing.

Printed in Canada

1 3 5 7 9 10 8 6 4 2

The suggestions and information contained in this publication are generally consistent with the *Clinical Practice Recommendations* and other policies of the American Diabetes Association, but they do not represent the policy or position of the Association or any of its boards or committees. Reasonable steps have been taken to ensure the accuracy of the information presented. However, the American Diabetes Association cannot ensure the safety or efficacy of any product or service described in this publication. Individuals are advised to consult a physician or other appropriate health care professional before undertaking any diet or exercise program or taking any medication referred to in this publication. Professionals must use and apply their own professional judgment, experience, and training and should not rely solely on the information contained in this publication before prescribing any diet, exercise, or medication. The American Diabetes Association—its officers, directors, employees, volunteers, and members—assumes no responsibility or liability for personal or other injury, loss, or damage that may result from the suggestions or information in this publication.

♾ The paper in this publication meets the requirements of the ANSI Standard Z39.48-1992 (permanence of paper).

ADA titles may be purchased for business or promotional use or for special sales. To purchase more than 50 copies of this book at a discount, or for custom editions of this book with your logo, contact the American Diabetes Association at the address below, at booksales@diabetes.org, or by calling 703-299-2046.

For all other inquiries, please call 1-800-DIABETES.

American Diabetes Association
1701 North Beauregard Street
Alexandria, Virginia 22311

The Diabetic Chef® is a registered trademark of Christopher J. Smith and used with permission.

Library of Congress Cataloging-in-Publication Data

Smith, Chris, 1966-
 The diabetic chef's year-round cookbook / by Chris Smith.
   p. cm.
 Includes index.
 ISBN 978-1-58040-292-7 (alk. paper)
 1. Diabetes--Diet therapy--Recipes. I. Title.

 RC662.S578 2008
 641.5'6314--dc22

                2008001689

Contents

ACKNOWLEDGMENTS

I WOULD like to thank the many people who have worked with me over the years to communicate a healthy lifestyle: Shannon Armfield, Charlie Brown, Diane Butler, Sharon Burstein, Julia Martinusen, Andy and Linda Lonigro, Chris Kroger, Jason Goins, and Cory Rayborn.

Additional thanks are due to the folks at the American Diabetes Association, including Jewelyn Morris and Greg Guthrie.

Special thanks go out to my parents for their continued support and guidance.

Lastly, this book is dedicated to my wife, Kathie, and my two sons, Ryan and Evan.

"One who gains strength by overcoming obstacles possesses the only strength which can overcome adversity."—Albert Schweitzer

An Introduction to Flavor

THE CLASSROOM LESSON

A FEW years back, I walked into a classroom to teach a course on "diabetic" cooking. I like to start personally, so I began by introducing myself and describing why I call myself The Diabetic Chef. After that, I always like to ask a few questions.

"How many of you are afflicted with diabetes?" I asked.

Nearly half of the audience raised their hands.

"And what would you like to learn from this cooking class?" I asked next.

A man in the back of the room yelled out, "Food that actually has taste!" Everyone started laughing and clapping.

"Flavorful food," someone else said.

I love these interactions with my classes because it always reminds me of a few key points about cooking and eating healthily. First and foremost, the class drew people from all walks of life, not just those with diabetes. Of course, some of the people attending were relatives of people with diabetes, but a substantial portion of the audience just wanted to eat healthier meals and came to my class to learn how. Anyone and everyone can learn to cook healthier meals, and you don't have to

have diabetes to make this happen.

Second, I am always reminded of how people truly want food that tastes good! When people in my classes say that they want more taste and flavor in their meals, I ask them, "What are you eating now?"

People often laugh when I ask them this because it's funny, but it also gets to the point about eating healthily and eating well, which don't have to be different things. If you ask yourself what you're eating now that is flavorless, tasteless, and bland, you can begin to examine how you and your family are truly eating. Are you eating out or staying home? When you eat at home, are you making your food from scratch, does the meal come out of a box or bag, or is it from the frozen foods aisle at your local grocery store? How do you season your food? Do you salt your food and then taste? This line of questioning always leads back to our homes and into every kitchen. You have the power to make healthy, tasty food right there in your own home.

GETTING THE MOST FROM YOUR MEALS

How can we make food more flavorful and still be healthy?

If we look at the whole meal, it begins with fresh ingredients. There is no denying that fresh ingredients contribute to the overall flavor and texture of a dish. It all begins with making sure that the things you purchase are of the highest quality. Knowing the proper color, smell, and appearance of your ingredients will help you determine the quality and freshness of your foods.

Where you shop is also very important. I go to different markets for different products. So I buy fish from one store, meats at another, and produce at the local farmers market. All of this shopping takes some extra time but guarantees that I'll have the best products available for every meal I prepare.

Knowing about the different types and cuts of meats is very important. Trimming away excess fat is an easy way to make your meats healthier. When you are selecting meats, go with the leaner cuts because they are generally higher quality. Lean meats include loin or tenderloin and some game meats, such as buffalo, venison, or rabbit.

Oils and fats can make a dish taste great, but from a nutritional standpoint can easily push a meal outside of your meal plan. When dealing with oils and fats, I always shoot for balance and moderation.

How you prepare a meal is another thing to consider when you're making healthier meals. The cooking methods that you use are fundamental to developing flavor in the foods you prepare. Whether it's reducing a liquid or caramelizing onions, your techniques can contribute to the overall dish without the addition of salt or fat. Grilling, poaching, steaming, or roasting a meat or vegetable can bring flavor, aroma, and texture to your palate!

STOCK YOUR KITCHEN THE RIGHT WAY

If you're going to cook well, you need to be prepared and that starts with your kitchen. No one can cook well if they're unprepared, so here is a short list of the things that I think every kitchen should have. I'm not going to tell you to go out and buy the highest-priced cookware and kitchen gadgets you can find; instead, I'm going to give you a list of the essentials. Many of these items can be found in your local grocery store, and all can add more flavor and kick to your meals.

Whenever possible, try to purchase the highest-quality ingredients available; it does make a difference. Don't forget, though, that higher prices don't always mean higher quality. The best way to find out what you and your family like is to purchase two or three different varieties, prepare them in different pans, and do a taste test. This is great fun! Plus, it's simple to do, gets your family involved, and helps you identify what suits your palate.

When cooking, always try substituting and experimenting with these "stocked" ingredients. Doing so allows you to add your own distinct character and panache to classic recipes or to create new recipes for your family and friends. Be sure to experiment with lots of different flavors, so you can find what you like. You may be surprised by what your taste buds love!

Are you ready to bring exciting flavors into your kitchen? Let's go shopping!

Extra-virgin olive oil: This oil offers a beautiful, aromatic bouquet that ranges from nutty to herbal to floral. The flavor, color, and aromatic characteristics can vary greatly depending on region and growing conditions. It is excellent for cooking or for salads. Be sure to try different brands for subtle differences.

Canola and grapeseed oil: Used for cooking at high heat but doesn't add an assertive flavor.

Roasted (or toasted) sesame oil: Use sparingly in salad dressings, marinades, and sauces. It is usually added at the end of the cooking process to add flavor.

Vinegars: If used sparingly, vinegars are a wonderful addition to sauces and salad dressings. The most common vinegars are red and white wine vinegars. Here are some of my favorite vinegars.

    Balsamic vinegar: This must-have ingredient is traditionally from Modena in northern Italy, where it has been made since the Middle Ages. It can be expensive but is well worth the cost. Use it on salads, vegetables, and some meats.

    Champagne vinegar: This vinegar is more subtle and sophisticated, yet has a delicate flavor.

    Rice vinegar: Quite common in Asian cuisine, rice vinegar is mellow and mild. You can find varieties flavored with onions, ginger, and spices.

    Aged cherry vinegar: Aged in wooden caskets, this vinegar is warm, mellow, and well rounded. It is a beautiful addition to any cook's stock but can be expensive.

Essential spices: Cayenne pepper, chili powder, cinnamon sticks, cumin (ground), curry powder, mustard, nutmeg, paprika, and whole peppercorns (black, white, and Szechwan).

Essential dried herbs: Bay leaves, dill, basil, oregano, rosemary, thyme, and sage.

Canned plum tomatoes

Dried pasta: Pick your favorite shapes and try some new ones.

Dried beans: Having beans handy is a great way to add a little more to those homemade dishes. Just remember that you'll have to soak them in water before using them.

Chicken and beef broth/stock: Always have this handy. You can either make your own and freeze it or keep a high-quality commercial brand nearby.

Essential fresh ingredients: Lemons, limes, oranges, garlic, onions, shallots, carrots, tomatoes, potatoes, mushrooms (try shiitake or Crimini, better known as baby Portobello), butter (salt free), sour cream (fat free), half & half (fat free), eggs, hard cheeses (Parmesan, Romano, or aged Gouda), mustard (grain, Dijon), capers, and olives.

EAT WELL, YEAR ROUND

Because healthy eating and daily living sometimes don't go hand in hand, I've developed this cookbook to bring easy meals into your home. It is always best to cook with fresh ingredients, so the cookbook is divided into pairs of months. By following this cookbook year-round, you'll guarantee that your meals are made from fresh, in-season ingredients. I've also made sure that each chapter has about the same number of recipes, so you'll be able to experience robust, healthy meals throughout the year. Getting ingredients that are in season will not only bring fresh recipes into your kitchen, but it'll also make you more aware of what and how you eat. Imagine how exciting it will be to have some favorite dishes back on your table when their ingredients come back in season!

You'll see that the first chapter of this book covers what I like to call *template cooking*. By using template cooking, you'll be able to harness your inner chef and make tasty, healthy, unique dishes on the fly. Template Cooking gives you the opportunity to exchange ingredients but still use the same cooking method. This allows you to develop skills on that particular cooking method while enjoying the diversity of ingredients you can substitute. I like to consider template cooking as an important lesson in learning how to cook well and healthily. That's why

it's the first chapter. The second chapter covers sauces, gravies, stocks, and sides. You'll be using these quick recipes with almost every meal, so it'll be handy to have them close at hand and easy to find.

For ease of use and versatility, recipes for breakfast and lunch are included in one chapter: "Starting Things Right: Breakfast & Lunch." Most of these recipes use ingredients that are available fresh throughout the year, so you won't need to spend a lot of time searching throughout the book for new and tasty breakfast and lunch dishes. And, after learning about template cooking, you'll be able to personalize many of these recipes to suit your and your family's tastes.

Remember, the recipes in this book are designed for people who want to eat well and live a healthy lifestyle, not just those with diabetes. The entire family should enjoy your meals, and I've designed these recipes to make everyone at the table smile. There's no reason why you shouldn't want to share your cooking with your family and friends, so don't let the idea of healthy cooking get you off track. The bottom line, as always, is to *enjoy your food*!

Chris Smith, The Diabetic Chef®
Visit my website at *www.thediabeticchef.com*

TIPS & TRICKS FROM THE DIABETIC CHEF®

COOKING LIKE a pro isn't hard to do, but some things can be tricky at the beginning. Here are some of my best tips for bringing tasty meals to your table. Following these tips will ensure that your dishes are flavorful, healthy, and worry free.

General Tips for Food and Cooking

Fresh herbs are a great addition to recipes. You should add most fine herbs at the end of the cooking process to release their delicate flavors and aromatic qualities. Their flavor usually diminishes the longer they are cooked, so be sure to add them later. Most thin, leafy herbs are in this category.

More hearty fresh herbs are more flexible and can withstand longer cooking times. They are great additions to soups, stews, and crock pot dishes. Examples of these include rosemary and sage.

Dried herbs should be added at the beginning of the cooking process. When you begin to cook (for example, a tomato sauce), you should add the oregano and basil beforehand so they can absorb the moisture and release their flavors into the sauce.

Always cook meats to temperature, not to time! Undercooked meats can be dangerous. Buy a meat thermometer; you'll love yourself for it.

When using wooden skewers, soak them in water for 30 minutes beforehand so they won't burn.

When you've finished cooking meat, remove it from the heat and let rest for 2–3 minutes. This allows the juices to settle, providing a juicier final product.

When cooking fish, reduce the heat by 25%. High heat will dry out fish.

Keeping Your Grill Shipshape

Keeping your barbecue grill in top shape is essential for good BBQ, so follow these steps for grill maintenance to make sure that it is safe, your food is fresh, and your BBQ flavors knock people out!

Remove the grill racks, lava rocks, and the burner assembly and set aside.

Use a wire brush and warm, soapy water to clean out the inside of the grill.

While the burner assembly is out, clean off all rust and corrosion with a wire brush and carefully inspect for clogged burner holes. Reassemble grill and test to make sure the flames spread evenly over the surface of the burner.

Remove leftover foods stuck to the racks by covering the racks with aluminum foil and running the grill on high for about 10 minutes. The baked-on food will turn into a fine white powder that can be brushed away.

Check the lava rocks for signs of wear. If they are cracked or starting to collect grease and to minimize "flare-ups," *change your lava rocks once a season or when they become saturated with barbecue liquids.* You can also use ceramic or porcelain briquettes that are available in most home improvement stores. These briquettes are less porous and can be baked clean by turning them over and heating them.

After using the grill, always clean the grates with a stiff wire brush. For porcelain-coated surfaces, use a brass bristle brush. For cast-iron surfaces, use a stainless steel wire brush.

Eat in Just 30 Minutes

Plan your meals a week in advance, so you don't have to frantically figure out what you're going to eat at 4:00 p.m.

Plan bigger meals for days when you have more time to prepare them. Plan easy meals when you have less time, so you can prepare them quickly.

Become a taskmaster. Give everyone in the household a role in preparing meals, whether it's buying groceries, thawing meats, or doing some prep work like chopping vegetables.

Decide which recipes you'll cook for the week beforehand. Not only will you have your meals for the week, but you'll also have your shopping list!

Practice what I like to call **Nutritional MVP** for managing meal plans. It stands for **Moderation**, limiting the amount of food you eat; **Variety**, eating different foods year-round and on your plate at every meal; and **Portion Control**, watching the amount and size of each portion of food you eat.

Use quick and simple cooking methods, such as sautéing, grilling, broiling, roasting, steaming, poaching, or submersion cooking.

Make sure that all meats and fish are fully and properly defrosted. Meats should be placed on a dish in your refrigerator up to two days to allow defrosting. Larger cuts of meat may take up to four days to defrost.

Select vegetables that are fresh and in season. Frozen vegetables are a good choice, but check the dates for freshness. If you use canned vegetables, drain them and rinse with cool water first. This helps remove excess salt and any metallic taste. Fresh vegetables are easy and fast to cook. Try beans, tomatoes, carrots, onions, leaf vegetables, asparagus, corn, broccoli, cauliflower, and peppers.

Try different starches. There are many different kinds of rice. Wild rice takes the longest to prepare, but is well worth the wait. Beans need to be soaked in water overnight to rehydrate. Because this can take many hours, it is best to soak and cook them the day before, and then you simply reheat them later. Pasta can also be cooked a day in advance and stored covered for up to two days in the refrigerator. Potatoes can be sliced and stored in water overnight. They can also be cooked the day before but should be served within 24 hours.

Meats will cook faster if you cut them into smaller pieces or thinner strips.

Quickly prepare shrimp, scallops, shellfish, and individual cuts of fish by sautéing, grilling, broiling, baking, or poaching. You can even put seafood on kabobs.

Herbs: Tidbits on Tarragon

Fresh tarragon leaves can be used either whole or chopped.

Tarragon goes well when minced in foods that include eggs, butter, marinades, vinegars, and sauces.

Fines herbes is a traditional French blend of four herbs: tarragon, chervil, chives, and parsley.

Dried tarragon leaves quickly lose their flavor and tend to taste like dry grass.

Place dried stems into a grill to "quick smoke" your food with the flavor of tarragon. This can work very well with fish and some vegetables.

Herbs: Basics on Basil

There are many varieties of basil, differing in shape, size, color, and flavor. All can be used in cooking.

Basil goes with most foods but pairs especially well with tomatoes, olive oil, and certain cheeses.

Basil leaves can be served whole, torn, *chiffonade* (when herbs are cut evenly into long, thin strips), chopped, minced, or pureed (as in pesto).

A simple pesto recipe uses fresh basil leaves, extra-virgin olive oil, fresh garlic, cheese, and pine nuts.

Herbs: Check on Chives

Chives are the smallest members of the onion family.

Fresh stems are long, hollow, and grasslike, with a rich dark green color.

Chives are delicate in flavor, so they should be added at the end of cooking to preserve character and flavor.

You can use fresh, frozen, or dried chives in your recipes.

This versatile herb works well in soups, salads, and sauces.

Chives are an herb in the traditional French blend, *fines herbes.*

Check in with Chicken

Purchase whole chickens and butcher them yourself. It's cost-effective, and you get two breasts, two thighs, two legs, and two wings in one package. Don't forget that you can use the carcass for chicken stock, too.

Always cook poultry to an internal temperature of 165°F.

When cooking chicken, use low to moderate heat to produce a moist, juicy chicken.

Cook chicken with the skin on and then remove the skin before serving. The skin acts as a natural jacket, protecting the tender meat from drying out and keeping the natural juices in.

Chickens in the grocery store are normally 5–8 weeks old.*

Americans consume 8 billion chickens a year.*

Alektorophobia is the fear of (usually only live) chickens.*

*From *10,001 Food Facts, Chefs' Secrets & Household Hints*, by Dr. Myles H. Bader. Northstar Publishing, 1998, p. 272–282.

Know Your Poultry

Free-range chickens are allowed to forage for food and consume a well-balanced diet. Their cage doors must be kept open according to USDA rules, and the chickens are usually sold whole.

Organic chickens must be raised on land that has not had any chemical fertilizer or pesticide used on it for at least three years. They must also be fed chemical-free grains and are generally also free-range chickens.

Mass-produced chickens are commercially raised in crowded coops and never allowed to run free.

Kosher chickens have been slaughtered and cleaned in compliance with Jewish dietary laws.

Broilers/fryers are 7-week-old birds that weigh 3–4 lbs.

Roasting chickens are usually hens that weigh 5–8 lbs with more fat than broilers.

Stewing hens are usually 4–8 lbs and are a year old. The meat is tough and needs to be slow cooked. They are generally more flavorful.

Capons are castrated roosters that are on average 10 weeks old and weigh 8–10 lbs. They usually have large white-meat breasts from making a lot of noise.

Poussins are baby chicks, only one month old, and weigh about 1 lb.

Cornish hens are baby chicks that are 5–6 weeks old and weigh about 2 lb. They are best when grilled or roasted.

Healthy Meals on a Deadline

I HAVE made it my personal mission to teach America how to cook healthily. Most Americans struggle with the amount of time required to prepare any meals at home, let alone healthy ones. Because of that, Americans are eating out more and more. This might be why Americans as a group are gaining weight. Is this true? I don't think that we can lay all of the blame at the steps of restaurants and fast food, but this does bring up a simple question: if we eat at home rather than eat out or order take out, will we necessarily be eating any healthier?

Over the years, I've asked this question countless times. I believe that you control the food, not the other way around. By preparing your meals at home, you have a better idea of the amount of salt, sugar, and fat that you're taking in. You also have more control over your portion sizes. And let's not forget that by preparing meals at home, you can save a lot of money. Can you do these things while eating out, too? Of course you can, but it's a whole lot easier to do it in your own kitchen.

So the challenge here is simple: build a week's worth of meals that you can realistically expect to afford, enjoy, and still have the time to cook. For well-balanced meals, I like to have a protein, a starch, and two vegetables. But before you ever start something new (exercise or a diet), check with your health care provider or dietitian to make sure you do it safely. So check with your health care team before you make changes to your diet in any way.

When it comes to planning meals, there are some things to keep in mind. Here they are.

First, people always seem to forget about texture and flavor when they are cooking. These are key components to a good meal, so always give texture and flavor a little thought when you plan meals. They should complement each other, not just taste the same. For example, why do people grill both their vegetables and meats with the same marinade? The food all tastes the same! You can avoid this by simply grilling your vegetables separately. This often happens when preparing foods quickly, but if you have a plan and are organized, you can have satisfying meals day after day.

Next, think about the color and balance of the foods you'll be preparing. How attractive is a plate that has only brown items? If you plan to have chicken every day, I bet you're going to hate it by Friday. You've got tons of options out there: beef, pork, poultry, lamb, veal, seafood, vegetables, pasta, and vegetarian choices. Try picking a different one for each day or plan a few days between the same foods. The idea is to offer simple but realistic meals that you can prepare and enjoy.

Build your week of meals and stick to that plan for the week. Use any recipe you like. There are tons of places where you can get recipes, including cookbooks, newspapers, magazines, and even your family cookbook. One thing that people do that is often very successful is to spend one day over the weekend cooking and freezing all the food they'll eat over the next seven days. A lot of people find this very convenient. But, if you have the time to cook each evening, you will have meals that are fresher and tastier.

There are a lot of perks to having weekly meal plans. You'll likely save time and money. Even more, you'll be able to enjoy the company of your family at the table every night. I find that this alone is an incentive, because I love spending time eating with my family. The amazing thing to me is that just a simple meal can bring families a little closer.

In the end, you will likely find that effective meal planning offers you the opportunity to be creative in the kitchen. You'll notice that cooking at home lets you control the food and the portions you eat. You will save money. Most important, eating regular meals will give you a chance to enjoy the company of your loved ones and catch up on the day's events. Make a dinner date, schedule time, and enjoy the people you love most!

TEMPLATE COOKING

TEMPLATE COOKING is a very simple idea. Basically, you have one recipe that can be prepared with different ingredients, but using the same techniques and cooking methods. In my travels I have met many people who want simple meals to prepare but want great taste, too. It occurs to me that all people want this from their food, too, so

I created these template recipes: Simple Chicken Breast and Maple Carrots.

SIMPLE CHICKEN BREAST

Let's start with the Simple Chicken Breast. You can replace the chicken with pork chops, steak, turkey cutlets, or even fish. You can even exchange the herbs and

---

SIMPLE CHICKEN BREAST

SERVES 4   SERVING SIZE: 1 BREAST HALF

4 CHICKEN BREASTS (4 OZ EACH)

1 TBSP EXTRA-VIRGIN OLIVE OIL

1 TSP DRIED ROSEMARY

1 TSP POULTRY SEASONING

1 TSP SALT-FREE LEMON PEPPER

1 TBSP MINCED GARLIC

1/2 TSP RED PEPPER FLAKES

COOKING SPRAY

1. In a medium bowl, combine all ingredients. Cover and refrigerate for 1 hour.

2. Preheat oven to 375°F.

3. Preheat sauté pan to medium-high heat. Spray pan with cooking spray. Add chicken breast to pan and sear to desired color, about 10 seconds, then turn over and sear other side.

4. When both sides are seared, remove chicken from pan and place in a baking dish or cookie sheet. Do not cover. Place in oven. Cook meat until it is done, at 165°F internal temperature. When chicken is done, remove from oven, and let rest for 2–4 minutes.

Exchanges/Choices

3 Lean Meat

1/2 Fat

Basic Nutritional Values

Calories 165
 Calories from Fat 55
Total Fat 6 g
 Saturated Fat 1.3 g
 Trans Fat 0 g
Cholesterol 65 mg
Sodium 60 mg
Total Carbohydrate 1 g
 Dietary Fiber 0 g
 Sugars 0 g
Protein 24 g

spices. The key to this recipe is how you prepare it. Key steps include marinating, preheating the pan, searing, finishing in the oven, cooking meat to temperature instead of time, and letting the meat rest. Every one of these steps contributes to a finished product that is fully cooked, juicy, and tender and, above all, has wonderful taste.

How This Template Works

Marinating: We're all searching for ways to bring more flavors to our foods. Marinating can do that. The ingredients in Simple Chicken Breast aim for a specific flavor, but not for any particular cuisine or dish. Instead, the Simple Chicken Breast recipe offers a taste that is fresh and flavorful, with hints of herbs, citrus, and spice. The extra-virgin olive oil adds a dimension to the flavor and also allows the herbs and spices to reach their full flavor.

Preheating and searing: This is so important because preheating allows you to sear the meat and searing results in caramelization, or browning. These simple techniques provide great flavor without adding any fat to your dishes! What is even better is that you can sear any meat and any cut. Chicken breasts, whole turkeys, pork chops, and leg of lamb; all of these can be seared. Searing enables you to control the look of the finished food and add flavor that would be lost by cooking meat in the oven. Brown all of the sides of the meat you're cooking to make sure that it is cooked evenly.

Cooking spray: Using cooking spray is an excellent way to cut down on the fat in your diet. Rather than pouring oil into your skillet, spraying gives you better control of the amount of fat you use.

Cook meats to temperature, not to time: This is a huge thing to remember whenever you cook meats. Making sure that your meats are cooked to the proper temperature is essential to safe, healthy, tasty food on your table. So when you've got a recipe that says "Cook for 15 minutes at 350°F," wait until your food is at the right temperature, not just until 15 minutes have passed. There's no guarantee that your oven is cooking at the temperature that you set the oven to, and an oven that is off by just 15°F can affect the foods you cook. I highly recommend that you go out and buy a meat thermometer right away. They are available at most grocery stores or specialty food stores.

USDA RECOMMENDED SAFE MINIMUM INTERNAL TEMPERATURES
Beef, Veal, and Lamb (Steaks and Roasts): 145°F
Fish: 145°F
Pork: 160°F
Beef, Veal, and Lamb (Ground): 160°F
Egg Dishes: 160°F
Turkey, Chicken, and Duck (Whole, Pieces, and Ground): 165°F

A meat thermometer is easy to use. Make sure that your thermometer is clean, and when you think the meat is finished, stick it into the thickest part of the meat without touching bone or the pan (both would give an inaccurate reading). Allow the thermometer to sit for a minute so it registers the correct temperature. When the meat is the proper temperature, it's done cooking.

It's generally good to place your meats on a wire rack in baking dishes in the oven. This ensures that your meat will be cooked evenly. If it sits at the bottom of the baking dish, the bottom of the meat will tend to be more cooked than the top. Also, by using a wire rack, the excess fat will drip off, leaving it in the pan and not on your meat.

Let it rest: Once the dish is removed from the oven, allow the meat to rest for a minute or two. This resting period allows the juices to settle back into your meat, which makes dishes a whole lot tastier.

MAPLE CARROTS

This template recipe teaches you how to do two essential things when cooking: reviewing and adjusting ingredient lists and reducing liquids to enhance flavor.

How This Template Works

Review and adjust ingredient lists: Notice that this recipe does not really need the extra salt and sugar, so if you want, you can take it out. Also, maple syrup vinegar is difficult to

---

MAPLE CARROTS

SERVES 4   SERVING SIZE: 1/4 RECIPE

8 OZ BABY CARROTS

WATER

1/2 TSP SALT (OPTIONAL)

1/2 TSP WHITE PEPPER

1 TBSP SUGAR (OPTIONAL)

2 TBSP MAPLE SYRUP VINEGAR

1. Place carrots in a shallow pan and add enough water to cover the carrots. Add the salt (optional), white pepper, sugar (optional), and maple syrup vinegar; bring to a simmer.

2. Simmer until liquid is completely reduced to a syrupy consistency. Serve immediately.

Exchanges/Choices
2 Vegetable

Basic Nutritional Values
Calories 35
Calories from Fat 0
Total Fat 0 g
Saturated Fat 0 g
Trans Fat 0 g
Cholesterol 0 mg
Sodium 40 mg
Total Carbohydrate 9 g
Dietary Fiber 2 g
Sugars 6 g
Protein 1 g

find in many stores. This happens pretty often when you're cooking from recipes. So, what should you do when you can't find an ingredient? You substitute, and for this recipe, you can use regular maple syrup. By substituting with maple syrup, you are adding a more complex flavor that has depth, richness, and sweetness. But maple syrup also adds carbohydrate, so you'll have to use about half as much as indicated for maple syrup vinegar (1 Tbsp). You'll want to do that anyway, because the syrup itself is more powerfully flavorful.

However, you can also use sugar-free maple syrup. See how ingredient substitutions work? It's easy!

Reducing liquids to enhance flavor: A lot of restaurants reduce their chicken or beef stocks to create deep, full-flavored fortified stocks. You don't need a lot of this on your plate to taste the intensity that comes from the reducing process. The most important thing about this recipe is to learn how to reduce a liquid, and then you can add or substitute ingredients that will complement carrots.

Everyday Essentials: Sauces, Gravies, and Stocks

TURKEY GRAVY

SERVES 16
SERVING SIZE: 1/4 CUP

2   TBSP OLIVE OIL

1/2   CUP DICED CARROTS

1/2   CUP DICED CELERY

1   CUP DICED ONIONS

1/2   CUP WHEAT FLOUR

1   CUP WHITE WINE

4   LB TURKEY BONES, ROASTED

2   QUARTS CHICKEN STOCK (SEE RECIPE ON P. 24)

2   BAY LEAVES

2   SPRIGS ROSEMARY

2   SPRIGS THYME

2   SPRIGS SAGE

1   TSP WHOLE BLACK PEPPERCORNS

1. In a medium saucepan over medium heat, add oil, carrots, celery, and onions. Sweat them. Stir until they are lightly golden in color. Add wheat flour and stir, cooking flour slightly. Add white wine and deglaze; reduce liquid by one-third.

2. Add the turkey bones, chicken stock, bay leaves, herbs, and black peppercorns. Bring to a simmer. Reduce heat to a low simmer and let cook uncovered. Skim off any fat that rises to the top. Continue to cook, allowing liquid to reduce by one-third.

3. Strain liquid and reserve. Serve over biscuits or English muffins.

Exchanges/Choices
1/2 Fat

Basic Nutritional Values
Calories 40
  Calories from Fat 20
Total Fat 2 g
  Saturated Fat 0.3 g
  Trans Fat 0 g
Cholesterol 5 mg
Sodium 10 mg
Total Carbohydrate 3 g
  Dietary Fiber 0 g
  Sugars 0 g
Protein 2 g

Tips for the Kitchen

You can purchase turkey wings and thighs with bones to make roasted turkey bones. Remove meat and place bones in a baking dish. Preheat oven to 375°F. Roast bones with a little oil until golden brown in color, turning as needed. Remove bones when they are golden in color, about 90 minutes. This will give your gravy a deeper color and flavor.

MARINARA SAUCE

SERVES 12
SERVING SIZE: 1/2 CUP

4	LB FRESH TOMATOES	
	WATER	
1	TBSP OLIVE OIL	
2	TBSP MINCED GARLIC	
2	CUPS CHICKEN STOCK (SEE P. 24)	
1	TSP SALT	
1/2	TSP BLACK PEPPER	
2	TSP MINCED FRESH OREGANO	
1	TBSP MINCED FRESH BASIL	

Exchanges/Choices
1 Vegetable

Basic Nutritional Values
Calories 35
  Calories from Fat 15
Total Fat 1.5 g
  Saturated Fat 0.2 g
  Trans Fat 0 g
Cholesterol 0 mg
Sodium 200 mg
Total Carbohydrate 5 g
  Dietary Fiber 1 g
  Sugars 3 g
Protein 1 g

1. Core the tomatoes and cut an X into the bottom of each, just piercing the skin. Place tomatoes into boiling water for 10–30 seconds, then plunge them into a bowl of ice water. This makes it very easy to remove the tomato skins.

2. Discard the skins and cut the tomatoes in half. Using your fingers, remove the tomato seeds and discard. Cut the tomatoes into a medium dice; then place them in a container and set aside.

3. Heat a large skillet over medium heat. Add the olive oil and garlic and cook the garlic for just a few seconds. Do not brown the garlic.

4. Add the diced tomatoes and stir. Increase to medium-high heat and bring the tomato mixture to a simmer. Cook until liquid is reduced, about 10–15 minutes. Add chicken stock as needed to adjust consistency. Continue to cook until tomatoes are very soft. Keep adding chicken stock until sauce is the desired consistency. Add salt, black pepper, oregano, and basil. Remove the mixture from the stove and allow it to cool.

Tips for the Kitchen

You can place this marinara sauce into muffin cups and freeze them overnight. The next day, remove the sauce from the molds, wrap them individually in plastic wrap, and refreeze. Now you have sauce ready whenever you need it!

CRANBERRY SAUCE

3/4	CUP WATER
1	12-OZ BAG WHOLE CRANBERRIES
3/4	CUP SUGAR
1	WHOLE CINNAMON STICK
1	TBSP GRATED ORANGE RIND
1/4	CUP TOASTED PECANS, CHOPPED COARSE

SERVES 16
SERVING SIZE: 2 TBSP

1. In a medium pot, bring the water to a simmer. Add the cranberries, sugar, cinnamon stick, and orange rind.

2. Simmer for 5–7 minutes or until most cranberries pop. Remove the mixture from the heat and add chopped pecans. Allow it to cool.

3. Refrigerate overnight. Remove the cinnamon stick before serving. (This cranberry sauce can be served warm, but it is best if chilled overnight.)

Exchanges/Choices
1/2 Carbohydrate

Basic Nutritional Values
Calories 50
  Calories from Fat 15
Total Fat 1.5 g
  Saturated Fat 0.1 g
  Trans Fat 0 g
Cholesterol 0 mg
Sodium 0 mg
Total Carbohydrate 10 g
  Dietary Fiber 0 g
  Sugars 10 g
Protein 0 g

ENCHILADA SAUCE

1	TBSP CANOLA OIL
2	CLOVES GARLIC, MINCED
1	LB TOMATOES, DICED
1	SMOKED POBLANO PEPPER, MINCED
2	CUPS CHICKEN STOCK (SEE RECIPE ON P. 24)
1	TSP CHILI POWDER
1	TSP SALT

SERVES 16
SERVING SIZE: 1/4 CUP

Exchanges/Choices
Free Food

Basic Nutritional Values
Calories 15
   Calories from Fat 10
Total Fat 1 g
   Saturated Fat 0.1 g
   Trans Fat 0 g
Cholesterol 0 mg
Sodium 150 mg
Total Carbohydrate 2 g
   Dietary Fiber 0 g
   Sugars 1 g
Protein 0 g

1. Heat pan and add canola oil. Add garlic, diced tomatoes, poblano pepper (you can buy this canned in the store or smoke one yourself, just follow the instructions for roasted peppers on p. 29), chicken stock, and chili powder. Bring to a simmer and cook until tomatoes are very tender.

2. Puree tomato mixture and add salt. Keep sauce hot until needed for recipe. It can also be chilled and stored for up to 2 days or frozen for up to 1 month.

Tips for the Kitchen

For additional heat, you can use jalapeño or Serrano peppers. Be careful, though, because these peppers can be hot!

BROWN STOCK

5	LB BEEF BONES
8	OZ ONIONS, LARGE DICE
4	OZ CARROTS, LARGE DICE
4	OZ CELERY, LARGE DICE
1	LB LEAN BEEF, MEDIUM DICE
6	OZ TOMATO PASTE
8	QUARTS WATER
4	CLOVES GARLIC
2	BAY LEAVES
2	SPRIGS FRESH ROSEMARY
10	SPRIGS FRESH THYME
1	TSP WHOLE PEPPERCORNS

SERVES 16
SERVING SIZE: 1 CUP

1. Preheat oven to 375°F.

2. Place bones, onions, carrots, and celery in a large roasting pan and cook in oven until bones reach a golden brown. Remove excess fat and transfer mixture to a large stockpot.

3. Add the beef and remaining ingredients to the stockpot and bring to a simmer. Gently skim off excess fat and scum from the surface. Simmer on low heat until reduced by half or until about 1 gallon of liquid remains. Strain liquid with a fine mesh strainer and cool immediately. Can be portioned and stored in the freezer.

Exchanges/Choices
Free Food

Basic Nutritional Values
Calories 15
  Calories from Fat 0
Total Fat 0 g
  Saturated Fat 0.1 g
  Trans Fat 0 g
Cholesterol 5 mg
Sodium 20 mg
Total Carbohydrate 2 g
  Dietary Fiber 0 g
  Sugars 0 g
Protein 2 g

Tips for the Kitchen

If you want to try them, veal bones, knuckles, and other trimmings can add additional flavor to your stocks.

BROWN SAUCE

SERVES 16
SERVING SIZE: 1/4 CUP

2	LB BEEF BONES (OR VEAL BONES)
8	OZ ONIONS, LARGE DICE
4	OZ CARROTS, LARGE DICE
4	OZ CELERY, LARGE DICE
2	QUARTS BROWN STOCK (SEE RECIPE ON P. 21)
6	OZ TOMATO PASTE
2	BAY LEAVES
2	SPRIGS FRESH ROSEMARY
10	SPRIGS FRESH THYME
1	TSP WHOLE PEPPERCORNS
3	OZ ARROWROOT
1/4	CUP WATER

Exchanges/Choices
1/2 Carbohydrate

Basic Nutritional Values
Calories 40
  Calories from Fat 0
Total Fat 0 g
  Saturated Fat 0.1 g
  Trans Fat 0 g
Cholesterol 5 mg
Sodium 20 mg
Total Carbohydrate 8 g
  Dietary Fiber 1 g
  Sugars 0 g
Protein 2 g

1. Preheat oven to 375°F.

2. Place bones, onions, carrots, and celery in a large roasting pan and cook in the oven until bones are golden brown in color. Remove excess fat.

3. Transfer mixture to a large stockpot. Add brown stock, tomato paste, bay leaves, rosemary, thyme, and peppercorns. Bring to a simmer and reduce liquid by one-third, about 1 hour. Strain liquid with a fine mesh strainer.

4. Bring liquid to a simmer again. Gently skim off any excess fat and scum from the surface.

5. In a small bowl, mix arrowroot and water to make slurry. In a steady stream, slowly pour the slurry into the brown sauce, whisking to incorporate. Allow to simmer. As soon as the sauce simmers, remove from heat and hold until needed. The arrowroot will thicken the brown sauce enough to coat the back of a spoon. Draw a line with your finger across the spoon and watch how the sauce drips down the line that you drew. This is a good indicator of how thick the sauce is and allows you to decide how you like your sauces.

BOURBON CRANBERRY SAUCE

2	TBSP OLIVE OIL
1/2	CUP DICED ONIONS
1/4	CUP DICED CARROTS
1/4	CUP DICED CELERY
1/2	CUP BOURBON
2	TBSP FLOUR
1/2	QUART CHICKEN STOCK (SEE RECIPE ON P. 24)
1/2	QUART BROWN SAUCE (SEE RECIPE ON P. 22)
2	BAY LEAVES
2	SPRIGS ROSEMARY
2	SPRIGS THYME
2	SPRIGS SAGE
1	TSP WHOLE BLACK PEPPERCORNS
1	CUP DRIED CRANBERRIES

SERVES 32
SERVING SIZE: 2 TBSP

Exchanges/Choices
1/2 Carbohydrate

Basic Nutritional Values
Calories 35
　Calories from Fat 10
Total Fat 1 g
　Saturated Fat 0.1 g
　Trans Fat 0 g
Cholesterol 0 mg
Sodium 5 mg
Total Carbohydrate 5 g
　Dietary Fiber 0 g
　Sugars 3 g
Protein 1 g

1. In a medium saucepot over medium heat, heat the oil. Add onions, carrots, and celery and sweat them until they are golden in color. Remove pot from the heat and deglaze with bourbon.

2. Add flour and stir to incorporate. Add chicken stock, brown sauce, and herbs and spices; bring to a simmer.

3. Continue cooking over a low simmer, skimming off fat and scum as it collects on top. Strain liquid and add cranberries. Hold until needed to serve.

FORTIFIED CHICKEN STOCK

SERVES 4
SERVING SIZE: 1 CUP

BOUQUET GARNI

5   LB CHICKEN BONES AND SCRAPS

8   QUARTS WATER

1   LB ONIONS, MEDIUM DICE

8   OZ CARROTS, MEDIUM DICE

8   OZ CELERY, MEDIUM DICE

Bouquet garni

2   BAY LEAVES

1   TSP BLACK PEPPERCORNS

1   SPRIG FRESH ROSEMARY

5   SPRIGS FRESH THYME

10 PARSLEY STEMS

Exchanges/Choices
(unfortified version
in parentheses)

1 Lean Meat (Free Food)

Basic Nutritional Values

Calories 30 (5)
  Calories from Fat 10 (0)
Total Fat 1 g (0 g)
  Saturated Fat 0.3 g (0.1 g)
  Trans Fat 0 g (0 g)
Cholesterol 15 mg (5 mg)
Sodium 25 mg (15 mg)
Total Carbohydrate 1 g (0 g)
  Dietary Fiber 0 g (0 g)
  Sugars 0 g (0 g)
Protein 4 g (1 g)

1. Wrap bouquet garni ingredients in a piece of cheesecloth and tie closed with culinary string or butcher's twine.

2. Put chicken bones and scraps, water, onions, carrots, celery, and bouquet garni in a large stockpot and bring to a simmer. Do not boil. Lower heat and continue to simmer for about 3 hours. Skim off fat and scum as it rises to the top.

3. Strain stock and allow it to cool. As stock chills, fat will collect on top; remove fat.

4. Return stock to the stovetop, bring to a boil and then back to a simmer, and reduce stock until about 1 quart remains. Allow stock to cool enough to safely divide it into portions for freezing.

5. Pour stock into storage containers and refrigerate or freeze until needed.

Tips for the Kitchen

This stock can be used to create soups and sauces and in any recipe that calls for chicken broth. In many of the recipes in this book, you can use this stock before it is fortified, which means that you stop the process at step 3 (the stock should be a golden color and have a light, delicate chicken flavor) and then divide it into portions and store it.

FISH STOCK

BOUQUET GARNI

5 LB FISH BONES AND TRIMMINGS

3 QUARTS COLD WATER

2 CUPS WHITE WINE

2 CUPS ONIONS, MEDIUM DICE

1 CUP CELERY, MEDIUM DICE

1/2 CUP SLICED MUSHROOMS

Bouquet garni

2 BAY LEAVES

1 TSP BLACK PEPPERCORNS

5 SPRIGS FRESH THYME

10 STEMS FRESH PARSLEY

SERVES 8
SERVING SIZE: 1 CUP

Exchanges/Choices
Free Food

Basic Nutritional Values
Calories 20
  Calories from Fat 0
Total Fat 0 g
  Saturated Fat 0 g
  Trans Fat 0 g
Cholesterol 5 mg
Sodium 10 mg
Total Carbohydrate 0 g
  Dietary Fiber 0 g
  Sugars 0 g
Protein 2 g

1. Wrap bouquet garni ingredients in a piece of cheesecloth and tie closed with culinary string or butcher's twine.

2. Rinse fish bones and trimmings; place in a large stockpot. Add the remaining ingredients (except bouquet garni) and bring to a simmer. Skim off fat that floats to the top and discard.

3. Add bouquet garni and simmer for 45 minutes to 1 hour, skimming off any additional impurities. Strain liquid. Use while hot or set aside to allow it to cool. Once cooled, this stock can be stored in smaller amounts and frozen for up to 3 months.

BOILED SHRIMP STOCK

4	CUPS WATER
1	WHOLE ONION
2	BAY LEAVES
6–8	PEPPERCORNS
1/2	LEMON
1	LB SHRIMP

SERVES 4
SERVING SIZE: 1 CUP

Exchanges/Choices
Free Food

Basic Nutritional Values
Calories 5
 Calories from Fat 0
Total Fat 0 g
 Saturated Fat 0 g
 Trans Fat 0 g
Cholesterol 5 mg
Sodium 15 mg
Total Carbohydrate 0 g
 Dietary Fiber 0 g
 Sugars 0 g
Protein 1 g

Bring water to a boil. Peel onion of outer skin and cut into quarters; place in boiling water. Add bay leaves, peppercorns, and lemon; bring to a simmer. Add shrimp and cook until shrimp are fully cooked, about 5–8 minutes (depending on size of shrimp). Remove shrimp and chill. Strain cooking liquid and hold until needed.

ASIAN-STYLE VINAIGRETTE

1	TBSP SESAME OIL
1/4	CUP RICE WINE VINEGAR
1/3	CUP CANOLA OIL
2	TSP MINCED FRESH GINGER
1	TSP MINCED FRESH GARLIC
1/2	TSP RED PEPPER FLAKES

SERVES 10
SERVING SIZE: 1 TBSP

1. In a medium bowl, combine the sesame oil and the rice vinegar, whisking to incorporate.

2. Pour canola oil into rice vinegar mixture, whisking until fully incorporated. Add the remaining ingredients and whisk to incorporate. Refrigerate for 2 hours or until ready to be served.

Exchanges/Choices
2 Fat

Basic Nutritional Values
Calories 80
  Calories from Fat 80
Total Fat 9 g
  Saturated Fat 0.7 g
  Trans Fat 0 g
Cholesterol 0 mg
Sodium 0 mg
Total Carbohydrate 0 g
  Dietary Fiber 0 g
  Sugars 0 g
Protein 0 g

ROASTED GARLIC

Exchanges/Choices
Free Food

Basic Nutritional Values
Calories 10
  Calories from Fat 5
Total Fat 0.5 g
  Saturated Fat 0.1 g
  Trans Fat 0 g
Cholesterol 0 mg
Sodium 0 mg
Total Carbohydrate 1 g
  Dietary Fiber 0 g
  Sugars 0 g
Protein 0 g

4   HEADS GARLIC (ABOUT 10 CLOVES EACH)
2   TBSP OLIVE OIL

1. Preheat oven to 350°F.

2. Cut off the very top of each garlic head and lay flat on a baking dish. Coat garlic heads with olive oil and place in the oven. Roast garlic until sides are soft, about 20–25 minutes. Remove from oven and allow to cool.

3. Allow the garlic to cool until safe to touch, then squeeze cloves to separate them from the head. Reserve until needed. Roasted garlic can be frozen in an airtight container for up to 3 months.

ROASTED RED PEPPERS

4   RED BELL PEPPERS

Place peppers over an open flame and scorch. Turn and roast peppers until outer skin is blackened, with blistering on all sides. Remove and immediately place in a bowl; cover with plastic wrap. Let cool for 10 minutes. Peel away burnt skin; remove stem and seeds. Pat dry with a paper towel and serve.

SERVES 8
SERVING SIZE: 1/2 PEPPER

Exchanges/Choices
1 Vegetable

Basic Nutritional Values
Calories 20
  Calories from Fat 0
Total Fat 0 g
  Saturated Fat 0 g
  Trans Fat 0 g
Cholesterol 0 mg
Sodium 0 mg
Total Carbohydrate 4 g
  Dietary Fiber 1 g
  Sugars 3 g
Protein 1 g

Tips for the Kitchen
Wrap roasted peppers in plastic wrap and store in an airtight container. The peppers will store well for 3 months in the freezer.

MANGO VINAIGRETTE

SERVES 24
SERVING SIZE: 1 TBSP

1	CUP VERY RIPE MANGOS, PEELED AND DICED
1/4	CUP RICE WINE VINEGAR
2	TSP MINCED FRESH GINGER
3	TBSP CANOLA OIL
1	TBSP MINCED CHIVES
	PINCH SALT
	PINCH PEPPER

Place diced mango, rice wine vinegar, ginger, and canola oil in a blender or food processor and blend until smooth. Add chives and season with salt and pepper. Refrigerate until needed.

Exchanges/Choices

1/2 Fat

Basic Nutritional Values

Calories 20
  Calories from Fat 20
Total Fat 2 g
  Saturated Fat 0.1 g
  Trans Fat 0 g
Cholesterol 0 mg
Sodium 0 mg
Total Carbohydrate 1 g
  Dietary Fiber 0 g
  Sugars 1 g
Protein 0 g

TANGERINE VINAIGRETTE

1/4	CUP TANGERINE JUICE (OR ORANGE JUICE)
2	TBSP BALSAMIC VINEGAR
1	TBSP MINCED SHALLOTS
4	TBSP WALNUT OIL
1	TSP TANGERINE ZEST
1/2	TSP SALT
	PINCH BLACK PEPPER
1	TSP MINCED LEMON THYME (OR FRESH THYME)

SERVES 10
SERVING SIZE: 1 TBSP

Combine the tangerine juice, balsamic vinegar, and shallots. In a slow stream, whisk in the walnut oil. Then, gently whisk in tangerine zest, salt, pepper, and lemon thyme. Refrigerate until needed (this recipe will last 2–3 days in the refrigerator).

Exchanges/Choices
1 Fat

Basic Nutritional Values
Calories 55
  Calories from Fat 45
Total Fat 5 g
  Saturated Fat 0.5 g
  Trans Fat 0 g
Cholesterol 0 mg
Sodium 115 mg
Total Carbohydrate 1 g
  Dietary Fiber 0 g
  Sugars 1 g
Protein 0 g

REDUCED BALSAMIC VINEGAR

SERVES 8
SERVING SIZE: 2 TBSP

Exchanges/Choices
1 1/2 Carbohydrate

Basic Nutritional Values
Calories 110
  Calories from Fat 0
Total Fat 0 g
  Saturated Fat 0 g
  Trans Fat 0 g
Cholesterol 0 mg
Sodium 30 mg
Total Carbohydrate 22 g
  Dietary Fiber 0 g
  Sugars 19 g
Protein 1 g

---

1   QUART BALSAMIC VINEGAR

Simmer balsamic vinegar and reduce until you have 1 cup. Set aside to cool. Store until needed. Pour vinegar into a clean glass jar or sanitized bottle. Cover tightly and store in your pantry.

STARTING THINGS RIGHT: BREAKFAST & LUNCH

KEYS TO SUCCESS: BREAKFAST AND LUNCH

Although this book covers a lot of meals—including soups, sauces, vegetables, entrées, and desserts— breakfast and lunch meals are just as important. Breakfast is the key to starting your day on the right foot. There are plenty of breakfast foods out there. You can always choose from cereals, eggs, and fruit, but in this book I offer you some simple recipes that are quick to prepare and will hold your hunger at bay.

Smoothies have become very popular these days, so I've offered you some of my personal favorites. They're ready in an instant and oh so good! Do you ever get tired of those same old egg dishes? I know I do, so I've added a few egg recipes that require baking and skip the skillet. They are a lot of fun to prepare and the taste variations are limited only by your imagination.

You'll also find a few lunch items in this section. I know that not everyone is an early riser! Try the Grilled Monte Cristo on p. 46 or the Grilled Trout Sandwich on p. 49 for extraordinary flavor in just a matter of minutes. I think you'll enjoy eating them as much as you'll enjoy making them!

STRAWBERRY SMOOTHIE

12	OZ LOW-FAT VANILLA YOGURT
1	CUP STRAWBERRIES
1	BANANA
4	OZ LOW-FAT MILK
1	CUP ICE
1/4	TSP CINNAMON

SERVES 4
SERVING SIZE: 1/4 RECIPE

In a blender or food processor, combine all ingredients and serve.

Exchanges/Choices
1 Fruit
1 Fat-Free Milk

Basic Nutritional Values
Calories 130
  Calories from Fat 20
Total Fat 2 g
  Saturated Fat 1 g
  Trans Fat 0 g
Cholesterol 5 mg
Sodium 65 mg
Total Carbohydrate 25 g
  Dietary Fiber 2 g
  Sugars 20 g
Protein 5 g

CRUNCHY
PEACH SMOOTHIE

SERVES 4
SERVING SIZE: 1/4 RECIPE

12	OZ LOW-FAT VANILLA YOGURT
1 1/2	CUPS PEACHES
4	OZ LOW-FAT MILK
1	CUP ICE
1/2	CUP WHEAT GERM

Exchanges/Choices
1/2 Starch
1/2 Fruit
1 Fat-Free Milk
1/2 Fat

Basic Nutritional Values
Calories 165
  Calories from Fat 25
Total Fat 3 g
  Saturated Fat 1.2 g
  Trans Fat 0 g
Cholesterol 5 mg
Sodium 65 mg
Total Carbohydrate 27 g
  Dietary Fiber 3 g
  Sugars 21 g
Protein 9 g

Blend yogurt, peaches, milk, and ice until smooth, about 1 minute. Pour wheat germ evenly over top to garnish. Serve immediately.

BLUEBERRY YOGURT SMOOTHIE

12	OZ LOW-FAT VANILLA YOGURT
1	CUP FRESH BLUEBERRIES
4	OZ LOW-FAT MILK
1	CUP ICE

SERVES 4
SERVING SIZE: 1/4 RECIPE

In a blender or food processor, combine all ingredients and serve.

Exchanges/Choices
1/2 Fruit
1 Fat-Free Milk

Basic Nutritional Values
Calories 110
  Calories from Fat 15
Total Fat 1.5 g
  Saturated Fat 1 g
  Trans Fat 0 g
Cholesterol 5 mg
Sodium 70 mg
Total Carbohydrate 19 g
  Dietary Fiber 1 g
  Sugars 18 g
Protein 5 g

BERRY ICE REFRESHER

SERVES 4
SERVING SIZE: 1/4 RECIPE

1	CUP STRAWBERRIES, CLEANED AND SLICED
1	CUP RASPBERRIES, WASHED
1	CUP BLUEBERRIES, WASHED
1/2	CUP APPLE JUICE
2	CUPS ICE
	MINT LEAF (OPTIONAL)

In a blender, combine strawberries, raspberries, blueberries, apple juice, and ice. Blend until smooth. Garnish with mint and serve.

Exchanges/Choices
1 Fruit

Basic Nutritional Values
Calories 65
  Calories from Fat 0
Total Fat 0 g
  Saturated Fat 0 g
  Trans Fat 0 g
Cholesterol 0 mg
Sodium 0 mg
Total Carbohydrate 15 g
  Dietary Fiber 4 g
  Sugars 10 g
Protein 1 g

Low-Fat Turkey Sausage Gravy

10   OZ TURKEY SAUSAGE PATTIES, CHOPPED

1/4   CUP ONIONS, SMALL DICE

  2   TBSP FLOUR

  2   CUPS FAT-FREE HALF & HALF

   DASH PEPPER

SERVES 12
SERVING SIZE: 1/4 CUP

1. Heat a medium saucepan; add turkey sausage patties and brown. When sausage is cooked, add diced onions and cook a few minutes, until onions are translucent.

2. Add flour to the sausage and onion mixture and stir to incorporate with the drippings, making a gravy. Simmer for just a minute or two, and then add the half & half, stirring to incorporate. Simmer for 5 minutes more, and season with pepper. Serve over biscuits or English muffins.

Exchanges/Choices
1/2 Carbohydrate
1 Fat

Basic Nutritional Values
Calories 90
  Calories from Fat 45
Total Fat 5 g
  Saturated Fat 1.4 g
  Trans Fat 0 g
Cholesterol 20 mg
Sodium 195 mg
Total Carbohydrate 5 g
  Dietary Fiber 0 g
  Sugars 2 g
Protein 5 g

OMELET WITH CHEDDAR AND LOW-FAT HAM

SERVES 1
SERVING SIZE: 1 OMELET

COOKING SPRAY
1/2 CUP EGG SUBSTITUTE
1 TBSP CHOPPED LOW-FAT HAM
2 TSP GRATED CHEDDAR

Exchanges/Choices
2 Lean Meat

Basic Nutritional Values
Calories 85
  Calories from Fat 15
Total Fat 1.5 g
  Saturated Fat 1 g
  Trans Fat 0 g
Cholesterol 10 mg
Sodium 325 mg
Total Carbohydrate 2 g
  Dietary Fiber 0 g
  Sugars 1 g
Protein 15 g

1. Preheat a nonstick pan to medium heat. Remove pan and quickly coat with cooking spray for 1 second. Place back on the heat; pour egg substitute into pan. Allow egg mixture to cook until almost done; add ham and press down, then flip and cook for 15 seconds.

2. Flip egg again, add cheese, and slide finished omelet onto a plate to serve.

Tips for the Kitchen

Add some more flavor to this tasty omelet with one or more of these optional additions: mushrooms, onions, peppers, tomatoes, fresh spinach, and herbs (chives, thyme, basil, oregano, or dill).

Zucchini and Mushroom Frittatas

1 TSP OLIVE OIL

1/2 CUP ZUCCHINI, MEDIUM DICE

1/2 CUP SLICED MUSHROOMS

PINCH BLACK PEPPER

COOKING SPRAY

1 CUP EGG SUBSTITUTE

2 TSP FRESHLY GRATED PARMESAN CHEESE

SERVES 2
SERVING SIZE: 1/2 RECIPE

1. Preheat a skillet and add olive oil. Sauté zucchini and mushrooms until they are slightly golden. Season with pepper. Set aside to cool, removing any excess liquid.

2. Using a different skillet, preheat and coat with cooking spray. Pour egg substitute into skillet, making sure that the skillet is evenly coated. Lower the heat and add the cooked vegetables on top. Be sure eggs are loose on the bottom of pan and that the vegetables are spread evenly.

3. When eggs are set, add Parmesan cheese and place under a broiler to finish cooking the top. Serve hot.

Exchanges/Choices
2 Lean Meat

Basic Nutritional Values
Calories 95
  Calories from Fat 25
Total Fat 3 g
  Saturated Fat 0.7 g
  Trans Fat 0 g
Cholesterol 0 mg
Sodium 250 mg
Total Carbohydrate 4 g
  Dietary Fiber 1 g
  Sugars 2 g
Protein 14 g

Spinach, Tomato, and Feta Cheese Baked Egg

Serves 4
Serving size: 1/4 recipe

Cooking spray
1/2 cup spinach, chiffonade
1/4 cup tomato, small dice
2 Tbsp fat-free feta cheese
1 tsp minced fresh oregano
4 medium eggs

Exchanges/Choices
1 Medium-Fat Meat

Basic Nutritional Values
Calories 75
 Calories from Fat 40
Total Fat 4.5 g
 Saturated Fat 1.4 g
 Trans Fat 0 g
Cholesterol 185 mg
Sodium 135 mg
Total Carbohydrate 1 g
 Dietary Fiber 0 g
 Sugars 1 g
Protein 7 g

1. Preheat oven to 375°F.

2. Spray 4 ramekins with cooking spray. Combine the spinach, tomato, feta cheese, and oregano; evenly distribute into ramekins. Place egg over spinach mixture and bake until egg whites are set but the yolks are still soft, about 10–12 minutes.

BAKED EGGS WITH VEGETABLES AND HERBS

COOKING SPRAY

1/2	CUP TOMATOES, SMALL DICE
1/4	CUP RED PEPPERS, SMALL DICE
1	TBSP SHALLOTS, SMALL DICE
1	TSP MINCED FRESH THYME
1	TSP MINCED FRESH TARRAGON
4	MEDIUM EGGS

SERVES 4
SERVING SIZE: 1/4 RECIPE

1. Preheat oven to 375°F.

2. Spray 4 ramekins with cooking spray. Combine the tomato, red peppers, shallots, thyme, and tarragon, and evenly distribute into ramekins. Crack each egg over the vegetable mixture in each ramekin.

3. Bake until egg whites are set but yolks are still soft, about 10–12 minutes.

Exchanges/Choices
1 Medium-Fat Meat

Basic Nutritional Values
Calories 75
  Calories from Fat 40
Total Fat 4.5 g
  Saturated Fat 1.4 g
  Trans Fat 0 g
Cholesterol 185 mg
Sodium 65 mg
Total Carbohydrate 2 g
  Dietary Fiber 1 g
  Sugars 1 g
Protein 6 g

Tips for the Kitchen

This dish is also known as *oeufs sur le plat*, in which the eggs are baked in individual dishes.

SPINACH AND EGG EN COCOTTE

SERVES 4
SERVING SIZE: 1/4 RECIPE

1 TBSP OLIVE OIL
6 OZ SPINACH
2 TBSP FORTIFIED CHICKEN STOCK (SEE RECIPE ON P. 24)
PINCH SALT
PINCH PEPPER
COOKING SPRAY
4 LARGE EGGS
4 WHOLE-WHEAT ENGLISH MUFFINS

Exchanges/Choices
2 Starch
1 Lean Meat
1 Fat

Basic Nutritional Values
Calories 250
Calories from Fat 90
Total Fat 10 g
Saturated Fat 2.3 g
Trans Fat 0 g
Cholesterol 210 mg
Sodium 415 mg
Total Carbohydrate 29 g
Dietary Fiber 5 g
Sugars 6 g
Protein 13 g

1. Preheat a sauté pan and add olive oil. Add spinach and chicken stock; quickly stir until spinach wilts. Season spinach with salt and pepper and then drain. Set aside.

2. Prepare 4 ramekins by spraying with cooking spray. Evenly portion spinach into each ramekin and then place or crack one egg over spinach in each ramekin. Cover each with foil. Place ramekins in a hot water bath and then put in a preheated 375°F oven. Bake until egg whites set and the yolks are still soft, about 20 minutes.

3. When eggs are done, serve in individual ramekins with a toasted English muffin on the side.

Tips for the Kitchen

Egg en cocotte is a fancy way of saying "eggs individually cooked in butter or cream in a ramekin." For this recipe, I reduced the amount of fat by using cooking spray. However, you can use a bit of melted butter to coat the ramekin; just be sure to remove any excess.

SWEET POTATO HASH

2	SWEET POTATOES
2	TBSP CANOLA OIL
1/2	CUP SLICED ONIONS
1/2	CUP SLICED RED PEPPERS
1	TSP SALT
1/2	TSP PEPPER
1/8	TSP CAYENNE PEPPER
1/2	TSP CINNAMON

SERVES 4
SERVING SIZE: 1/4 RECIPE

1. In a pot of boiling water, boil whole sweet potatoes until cooked but still firm, about 15–20 minutes. Remove skins and cut to a medium dice. Set aside.

2. Heat a large skillet and add 2 tsp canola oil. Sauté onions until lightly browned. Add red peppers and continue to cook. Remove from skillet and set aside. Add remaining canola oil and sweet potatoes to skillet. When sweet potatoes are browning, return onions and red peppers to skillet. Continue to cook until sweet potatoes have browned. Season with salt, pepper, cayenne pepper, and cinnamon. Serve immediately.

Exchanges/Choices
1 Starch
1 1/2 Fat

Basic Nutritional Values
Calories 145
  Calories from Fat 65
Total Fat 7 g
  Saturated Fat 0.6 g
  Trans Fat 0 g
Cholesterol 0 mg
Sodium 590 mg
Total Carbohydrate 19 g
  Dietary Fiber 2 g
  Sugars 5 g
Protein 1 g

This recipe is
high in sodium.

GRILLED MONTE CRISTO

SERVES 2
SERVING SIZE: 1 SANDWICH

4   TSP DIJON MUSTARD

1   TBSP REDUCED-FAT MAYONNAISE

4   SLICES WHOLE-WHEAT BREAD

3   OZ LEAN TURKEY, SLICED

2   OZ FRESH ROAST PORK, SLICED

1   OZ FAT-FREE SWISS CHEESE, SLICED

1/4   CUP LOW-FAT MILK

1/2   CUP EGG SUBSTITUTE

COOKING SPRAY

Exchanges/Choices
2 Starch
5 Lean Meat

Basic Nutritional Values
Calories 370
  Calories from Fat 90
Total Fat 10 g
  Saturated Fat 2.3 g
  Trans Fat 0 g
Cholesterol 60 mg
Sodium 905 mg
Total Carbohydrate 29 g
  Dietary Fiber 4 g
  Sugars 7 g
Protein 39 g

This recipe is
high in sodium.

---

1. Combine the mustard and mayonnaise; spread evenly over the bread. Layer sliced turkey, pork, and cheese evenly on two pieces of bread; cover with remaining two pieces.

2. In a separate bowl, combine the milk and egg substitute; beat until combined. Dip sandwich in egg batter and cook on a skillet, browning both sides. Slice in half and serve immediately.

Tips for the Kitchen

Make this sandwich taste even better by using a panini grill!

MINI PEPPERONI PIZZA

1	LB REFRIGERATED PIZZA DOUGH
1 1/2	CUPS MARINARA SAUCE (SEE RECIPE ON P. 18)
1	LB FAT-FREE MOZZARELLA CHEESE, GRATED
1 1/2	OZ PEPPERONI, SLICED THIN
2	TBSP FRESHLY GRATED PARMESAN CHEESE

SERVES 6
SERVING SIZE: 1 MINI PIZZA

1. Cut the pizza dough into six equal pieces. Mold the pieces of dough into individual thin pizza crusts. Spread a thin layer of marinara sauce over each pizza crust.

2. Spread a layer of mozzarella cheese evenly over each pizza. Top with the pepperoni and a sprinkle of Parmesan cheese.

3. Preheat oven to 400°F (with a pizza stone, if you have one). Bake for 7–10 minutes or until the bottom of the pizzas are golden brown. Remove the pizzas from the oven and let rest for 2 minutes before serving.

Exchanges/Choices
3 Starch
3 Lean Meat

Basic Nutritional Values
Calories 370
  Calories from Fat 65
Total Fat 7 g
  Saturated Fat 2.3 g
  Trans Fat 0 g
Cholesterol 20 mg
Sodium 1725 mg
Total Carbohydrate 44 g
  Dietary Fiber 1 g
  Sugars 6 g
Protein 30 g

This recipe is
high in sodium.

Open-Faced Cheese Melts

Serves 4
Serving size: 1 cheese melt

4	slices Italian bread (about 1 inch thick)
4	tsp Dijon mustard
1	Tbsp onions, small dice
4	oz fat-free Swiss cheese
4	oz extra-lean, lower-sodium ham, diced

Exchanges/Choices
1 1/2 Starch
2 Lean Meat

Basic Nutritional Values
Calories 180
  Calories from Fat 20
Total Fat 2 g
  Saturated Fat 0.5 g
  Trans Fat 0 g
Cholesterol 20 mg
Sodium 925 mg
Total Carbohydrate 24 g
  Dietary Fiber 1 g
  Sugars 4 g
Protein 15 g

This recipe is
high in sodium.

1. Preheat oven to 400°F.

2. Cut 1-inch-thick slices of Italian bread on an angle to get 4 longer slices (this is called a bias cut). Reserve the rest of the bread for another use.

3. Spread mustard evenly on bread. Add diced onion, cheese, and ham. Place on a baking sheet and bake until cheese melts. Remove and enjoy.

GRILLED TROUT SANDWICH

COOKING SPRAY

2 FILLETS FRESH TROUT (6 OZ EACH)

2 TBSP LEMON JUICE

FRESH GROUND PEPPER

1 TSP FRESH DILL, MINCED

2 TSP OLIVE OIL

4 KAISER ROLLS

4 TSP DIJON MUSTARD

4 LETTUCE LEAVES

4 TOMATO SLICES

4 ONION SLICES

SERVES 4
SERVING SIZE: 1 SANDWICH

1. Preheat grill. Spray grill with cooking spray so the fish will not stick. Season trout fillets with lemon juice, pepper, dill, and olive oil; marinate for 10 minutes.

2. Place fillets onto grill and wait for grill lines to mark the fish. Flip over and grill until fish is done.

3. Place fillet onto a fresh kaiser roll; add 1 tsp Dijon mustard, 1 lettuce leaf, 1 tomato slice, and 1 onion slice.

Exchanges/Choices

2 Starch

3 Lean Meat

1 Fat

Basic Nutritional Values

Calories 330
  Calories from Fat 100
Total Fat 11 g
  Saturated Fat 1.7 g
  Trans Fat 0 g
Cholesterol 50 mg
Sodium 480 mg
Total Carbohydrate 34 g
  Dietary Fiber 2 g
  Sugars 4 g
Protein 24 g

Turkey and Swiss Wrap

SERVES 2
SERVING SIZE: 1 WRAP

2   SPINACH WRAPS (10 INCH)

4   OZ 98% FAT-FREE ROASTED TURKEY, SLICED

2   OZ LOW-SODIUM SWISS CHEESE, SLICED

2   OZ LETTUCE

3   OZ TOMATO SLICES

2   OZ FAT-FREE RASPBERRY VINAIGRETTE

Exchanges/Choices
2 1/2 Starch
1/2 Carbohydrate
3 Lean Meat

Basic Nutritional Values
Calories 375
  Calories from Fat 55
Total Fat 6 g
  Saturated Fat 1.7 g
  Trans Fat 0.5 g
Cholesterol 55 mg
Sodium 1125 mg
Total Carbohydrate 49 g
  Dietary Fiber 3 g
  Sugars 13 g
Protein 30 g

This recipe is
high in sodium.

1. Place spinach wraps on a flat surface. Lay turkey evenly across the lower third of the wrap. Place cheese evenly on top of turkey. Add lettuce and tomato over Swiss cheese and drizzle vinaigrette over the lettuce and tomato.

2. Fold the lower lip of the wrap over the ingredients. Give it a good tuck and then begin to roll, tightening as you go along. When finished rolling, slice in half and serve immediately.

January

&

February

THREE PILLARS OF A HEALTHY LIFESTYLE

WHEN JANUARY and February roll around and the holiday season ends, it's time for new beginnings. This is a great time to identify improvements that you can add to your lifestyle. There are three areas that you can focus on: nutrition, physical fitness, and stress management. For years, my focus has been to manage these three areas and provide the same environment for my family. More importantly, having an awareness of these areas and a commitment to work toward personal goals are the keys to long-term success for yourself and your family.

I'm not a big fan of the word "diet" because of the negative connotations associated with it, so I like to look at it as managing your nutrition or food instead. I like to call healthy eating "Nutritional Management." It's not hard to add Nutritional Management to your schedule; simply put, it is a commitment to eating healthily. What foods you eat, how much of them you eat, the time of day that you eat, and the variety of foods you choose all play a role in your overall nutrition. "You are what you eat" has never been more true, so choose your foods wisely and before you know it you will be well on your way to better Nutritional Management.

Physical fitness begins simply, by bringing physical activity into your life. Before beginning any activity plan, see your doctor first to discuss what activities and level of activity you should follow. Next, sit down with your calendar and plan the time that you can commit to on a weekly basis, and stick with it! The hardest part of a new exercise routine is in the first 4–6 weeks. Work hard to stick with your plan through that time frame. You will find that after you've passed the first 6 weeks that you are on your way to a long-term overall healthier lifestyle.

Stress is difficult to identify, yet we tend to just deal with it. Often when I address an audience, I ask them to raise their hands if they feel that they are stressed out. Hands will slowly begin to raise, which is when I announce that "the rest of you are too stressed out to raise your hands!" With a bit of laughter, the point is acknowledged and we move on.

By no means am I an expert on stress, but I do feel that it is important to identify times when you are stressed and to acknowledge that you have stress in your life. When you do find that you get stressed out, think of ways to help you reduce the stress in your life. For some people, this might be a spiritual or meditative approach. For many people, simply adding some stretching or exercise makes the stress disappear. It is important to reduce the stress in your life because it makes you feel good and can help keep you focused on healthy goals.

SHRIMP COCKTAIL

2   QUARTS WATER

2   BAY LEAVES

2   TBSP OLD BAY SEASONING

1   ONION, LARGE DICE

1   LEMON, QUARTERED

1   LB RAW SHRIMP

1. Bring water to a boil and add all ingredients except the shrimp. Simmer for 2 minutes; then add shrimp. Cook until shrimp is fully cooked, about 4 minutes. You can check by breaking through a shrimp and seeing how cooked it is in the center. The shrimp should have firm white meat cooked all the way through the center.

2. Drain water and place shrimp into an ice bath to cool rapidly. Serve chilled with cocktail sauce (see recipe on p. 54).

Exchanges/Choices
1 Lean Meat

Basic Nutritional Values
Calories 55
  Calories from Fat 5
Total Fat 0.5 g
  Saturated Fat 0.2 g
  Trans Fat 0 g
Cholesterol 110 mg
Sodium 290 mg
Total Carbohydrate 0 g
  Dietary Fiber 0 g
  Sugars 0 g
Protein 12 g

COCKTAIL SAUCE

2	TBSP HORSERADISH, MINCED
1	LEMON
1/2	CUP KETCHUP
1/2	CUP CHILI SAUCE
1	TBSP WORCESTERSHIRE SAUCE
	PINCH BLACK PEPPER

SERVES 10
SERVING SIZE: 2 TBSP

Exchanges/Choices
1/2 Carbohydrate

Basic Nutritional Values
Calories 30
 Calories from Fat 0
Total Fat 0 g
 Saturated Fat 0 g
 Trans Fat 0 g
Cholesterol 0 mg
Sodium 335 mg
Total Carbohydrate 7 g
 Dietary Fiber 0 g
 Sugars 3 g
Protein 1 g

1. Wash and thoroughly dry horseradish. Cut or peel away the outer skin. Grate horseradish; then chop until it is very fine. Reserve.

2. Wash and dry lemon. Zest and juice the lemon and set aside.

3. Combine all ingredients. Refrigerate overnight before serving.

SPINACH STRUDEL

1	TBSP OLIVE OIL
1/2	CUP ONIONS, SMALL DICE
1	LB FRESH SPINACH, COARSELY CHOPPED
1/2	TSP SALT
1/2	TSP PEPPER
1	CUP LOW-FAT RICOTTA CHEESE
1/4	CUP FAT-FREE FETA CHEESE
1	TBSP FRESH OREGANO, MINCED
1	EGG
4	SHEETS PHYLLO DOUGH

SERVES 8
SERVING SIZE: 1/8 RECIPE

Exchanges/Choices
1/2 Starch
1 Vegetable
1 Lean Meat

Basic Nutritional Values
Calories 115
  Calories from Fat 40
Total Fat 4.5 g
  Saturated Fat 1.5 g
  Trans Fat 0 g
Cholesterol 35 mg
Sodium 395 mg
Total Carbohydrate 13 g
  Dietary Fiber 2 g
  Sugars 2 g
Protein 8 g

1. Heat olive oil in a large pan and sweat onions. Add spinach and cook until just wilted. Season with a pinch of salt and pepper; squeeze out excess liquid from spinach and drain. Set aside to cool.

2. In a separate large bowl, combine the ricotta cheese, feta cheese, oregano, egg, spinach mixture, and remaining salt and pepper. Set aside in the refrigerator.

3. Place two sheets of phyllo dough onto a clean work area and lightly brush with olive oil. Place two more sheets on top and brush with more olive oil. Evenly spread the spinach mixture down the center of the dough lengthwise. Fold one side over the mixture and under spinach filling. Tuck closed. Fold other side over top and, using a dab of olive oil, secure the sheet to the bottom of the strudel. Brush olive oil over the top and place on a baking sheet. With a sharp knife, cut slits on top. Place in a preheated 375°F oven and bake until golden brown, about 20–25 minutes.

4. When cooking is finished, allow strudel to cool, about 10 minutes. Using a sharp knife, cut the strudel into eight equal portions. Serve warm.

SHERRY MUSHROOM AND WILD RICE SOUP

SERVES 8
SERVING SIZE: 1 CUP

2	TBSP OLIVE OIL, DIVIDED
2	LB WHITE MUSHROOMS, COARSELY CHOPPED
1/2	CUP ONIONS, SMALL DICE
2	CUPS SHERRY
2	QUARTS CHICKEN STOCK (SEE RECIPE ON P. 24)
1	SPRIG ROSEMARY (ABOUT 1 INCH)
4	SPRIGS THYME
2	BAY LEAVES
1	LB SHIITAKE MUSHROOMS
1/2	CUP CORNSTARCH
5	TBSP WATER
1	CUP COOKED WILD RICE
1	CUP FAT-FREE HALF & HALF
1/4	CUP MINCED CHIVES

Exchanges/Choices

1 Carbohydrate
1 Fat

Basic Nutritional Values

Calories 145
  Calories from Fat 40
Total Fat 4.5 g
  Saturated Fat 0.8 g
  Trans Fat 0 g
Cholesterol 5 mg
Sodium 50 mg
Total Carbohydrate 19 g
  Dietary Fiber 1 g
  Sugars 4 g
Protein 4 g

---

1. Preheat a stockpot over medium heat. Add 1 Tbsp olive oil and white mushrooms and sauté. Add onions and continue to cook until onions are soft. Deglaze with sherry and reduce to a simmer. Reduce liquid by half; add chicken stock, rosemary, thyme, and bay leaves. Bring back to a simmer. Skim off excess fat or scum and continue to simmer on low heat for about 45 minutes. Remove pot from heat and strain liquid. Set liquid aside and discard the rest.

2. Preheat a clean pot. Add 1 Tbsp olive oil and sweat shiitake mushrooms until tender and golden in color. Add mushroom stock and bring to a simmer.

3. In a bowl, combine cornstarch and water to make slurry. Slowly pour cornstarch slurry into mushroom stock, whisking as you incorporate.

4. Add wild rice and bring to a simmer, then remove from heat. Whisk in half & half; garnish with chives. Serve immediately.

Tips for the Kitchen

To add complexity to this dish, use a variety of different mushrooms. You can sauté additional mushrooms and use them as a garnish.

CHICKEN TORTELLINI SOUP

SERVES 6
SERVING SIZE: 1/6 RECIPE

2 TSP OLIVE OIL

1 TBSP MINCED GARLIC

10 OZ WHOLE PLUM TOMATOES, PEELED AND CRUSHED BY HAND

1 QUART CHICKEN STOCK (SEE RECIPE ON P. 24)

1 CUP TORTELLINI PASTA

2 TBSP FRESH PARSLEY

1 TBSP FRESHLY GRATED PARMESAN CHEESE

1. Heat a medium stockpot over medium heat. Add olive oil and garlic; sweat slightly. Add crushed tomatoes and bring to a simmer. Continue cooking until liquid is almost completely reduced.

2. Add chicken stock and bring to a simmer. Add tortellini; cook until tortellini is done.

3. Remove from heat. Add parsley and serve garnished with Parmesan cheese.

Exchanges/Choices
1/2 Starch
1 Vegetable
1/2 Fat

Basic Nutritional Values
Calories 80
Calories from Fat 20
Total Fat 2.5 g
Saturated Fat 0.6 g
Trans Fat 0 g
Cholesterol 5 mg
Sodium 35 mg
Total Carbohydrate 12 g
Dietary Fiber 1 g
Sugars 1 g
Protein 3 g

CABBAGE AND NOODLES

SERVES 4
SERVING SIZE: 1/4 RECIPE

2	STRIPS BACON, DICED
1	CUP SLICED ONIONS
2	TBSP MINCED GARLIC
1	LB CABBAGE, CLEANED AND THINLY SLICED
1	CUP FORTIFIED CHICKEN STOCK (SEE RECIPE ON P. 24)
2	CUPS COOKED EGG NOODLES
1	TSP SALT
1/2	TSP PEPPER
1/4	CUP MINCED FRESH PARSLEY

Exchanges/Choices
1 1/2 Starch
2 Vegetable
1 1/2 Fat

Basic Nutritional Values
Calories 225
  Calories from Fat 70
Total Fat 8 g
  Saturated Fat 2.9 g
  Trans Fat 0 g
Cholesterol 35 mg
Sodium 695 mg
Total Carbohydrate 31 g
  Dietary Fiber 4 g
  Sugars 6 g
Protein 8 g

This recipe is
high in sodium.

1. In a stockpot, render bacon (this means to melt off the fat). Add onions and garlic and sauté. Add cabbage and fortified chicken stock. Slowly cook until cabbage is tender.

2. Add cooked egg noodles; season with salt and pepper. Garnish with fresh parsley and serve immediately.

SIMPLE BAKED HALIBUT

4   HALIBUT STEAKS (4 OZ EACH)
8   SPRIGS FRESH THYME
    PINCH SALT
    PINCH FRESH GROUND PEPPER
4   COIN-SHAPED LEMON SLICES

SERVES 4
SERVING SIZE: 1 HALIBUT STEAK

1. Preheat oven to 375°F.

2. Put steaks in a baking dish; season with thyme, salt, and pepper. Place a lemon slice on top of each steak. Cover dish, place in the preheated oven, and bake. Cook until fish is firm and begins to flake in the thickest part. Remove and serve immediately.

Exchanges/Choices
3 Lean Meat

Basic Nutritional Values
Calories 130
  Calories from Fat 20
Total Fat 2.5 g
  Saturated Fat 0.4 g
  Trans Fat 0 g
Cholesterol 35 mg
Sodium 60 mg
Total Carbohydrate 2 g
  Dietary Fiber 1 g
  Sugars 0 g
Protein 24 g

Black Bean and Roasted Vegetable Enchiladas

SERVES 8
SERVING SIZE: 1 ENCHILADA

2	LARGE EARS OF CORN, ROASTED
8	FLOUR TORTILLAS (10 INCHES EACH)
2	CUPS BLACK BEANS, COOKED
2	ROASTED RED PEPPERS, SEEDS REMOVED, SMALL DICE (SEE RECIPE ON P. 29)
1/2	CUP ONIONS, SMALL DICE
1/4	CUP CHILIES, SMALL DICE
12	OZ FAT-FREE CHEDDAR CHEESE, GRATED
	COOKING SPRAY
1	CUP ENCHILADA SAUCE (SEE RECIPE ON P. 20)

Exchanges/Choices
3 1/2 Starch
1 Vegetable
2 Lean Meat

Basic Nutritional Values
Calories 400
  Calories from Fat 65
Total Fat 7 g
  Saturated Fat 1.5 g
  Trans Fat 0 g
Cholesterol 10 mg
Sodium 945 mg
Total Carbohydrate 60 g
  Dietary Fiber 8 g
  Sugars 6 g
Protein 25 g

This recipe is
high in sodium.

1. Roast the corn. Soak corn and husks in water for 10 minutes. Place whole ears on a grill and cook, turning as husk browns. Cook evenly on all sides until done, about 10–12 minutes. Cut off corn kernels and set aside.

2. Preheat the oven to 375°F.

3. Evenly fill each tortilla with roasted corn, cooked black beans, roasted red pepper, onions, and diced chilies. Sprinkle cheese on top and roll up each tortilla. Spray a baking dish with cooking spray and arrange enchiladas in dish. Pour enchilada sauce over each tortilla and cover dish.

4. Bake until the sauce and cheese are bubbling around the edges of the dish. Remove cover; add any remaining cheese and allow cheese to melt. Serve hot.

SEAFOOD CASSEROLE

2	TBSP OLIVE OIL, DIVIDED
1	CUP LEEKS, CLEANED AND DICED
1	CUP MUSHROOMS, SLICED IN HALF
1	CUP GRATED CARROT
1	LB HALIBUT OR OTHER FIRM WHITE FISH
1/2	CUP WHITE WINE
12	CLAMS WITH JUICE
1	TBSP DILL
1/2	TSP BLACK PEPPER
4	CUPS COOKED BROWN RICE
3/4	CUP FRESHLY GRATED PARMESAN CHEESE

SERVES 6
SERVING SIZE: 1/6 RECIPE

1. In a medium stockpot, heat 1 Tbsp oil over medium-high heat. Add leeks and sweat them, stirring constantly. Add mushrooms; continue to cook, until just tender. Add carrots and gently sauté for 1 minute. Remove from pot and set aside.

2. Add remaining olive oil to a pan and cook halibut until just done. Add wine and clams with juice; bring to a simmer. Add vegetable mixture and combine. Add dill and pepper.

3. Add cooked brown rice and gently incorporate. Place in a casserole dish and top with cheese. Bake covered at 350°F until the casserole reaches an internal temperature of 160°F. Let rest for 5 minutes before serving.

Exchanges/Choices
2 Starch
1 Vegetable
3 Lean Meat
1 Fat

Basic Nutritional Values
Calories 375
  Calories from Fat 110
Total Fat 12 g
  Saturated Fat 3.1 g
  Trans Fat 0 g
Cholesterol 50 mg
Sodium 180 mg
Total Carbohydrate 35 g
  Dietary Fiber 3 g
  Sugars 3 g
Protein 31 g

PENNSYLVANIA DUTCH-STYLE CHOPS AND KRAUT WITH GRANNY SMITH APPLES

SERVES 4
SERVING SIZE: 1 CHOP

4	PORK CHOPS (6 OZ EACH), TRIMMED OF FAT
1	TSP SALT
	PINCH BLACK PEPPER
1	TBSP CANOLA OIL
16	OZ SAUERKRAUT, WITH LIQUID
1	MEDIUM ONION, JULIENNED
1	TBSP BROWN SUGAR
1/4	CUP RAISINS
2	MEDIUM GRANNY SMITH APPLES, CORED AND WEDGED

Exchanges/Choices
1 Fruit
2 Vegetable
3 Lean Meat
1 1/2 Fat

Basic Nutritional Values
Calories 310
  Calories from Fat 100
Total Fat 11 g
  Saturated Fat 2.9 g
  Trans Fat 0 g
Cholesterol 70 mg
Sodium 1385 mg
Total Carbohydrate 28 g
  Dietary Fiber 5 g
  Sugars 20 g
Protein 27 g

This recipe is
high in sodium.

---

1. Season pork chops with salt and pepper. Preheat a skillet and add canola oil. Sear pork chops until they are a golden color on both sides.

2. In a medium baking dish, layer the sauerkraut, onion, brown sugar, and raisins. Place browned pork chops on top and add sliced apples over pork chops. Cover and bake at 350°F for about 1 hour or until pork chops are tender. Remove pork chops when the meat is tender and pulls easily from the bone.

SHEPHERD'S PIE

1	LB 90% LEAN GROUND BEEF
1/2	CUP ONIONS, FINELY DICED
1	TBSP MINCED GARLIC
1	CUP BABY CARROTS, WASHED
1/2	CUP CELERY ROOT, SMALL DICE
1	TSP MINCED FRESH ROSEMARY
1	TSP MINCED FRESH THYME
1 1/2	CUPS BROWN SAUCE (SEE RECIPE ON P. 22)
3	CUPS EASY MASHED POTATOES (SEE RECIPE ON P. 182)

SERVES 8
SERVING SIZE: 1 SLICE

1. Preheat oven to 350°F.

2. In a medium nonstick skillet, brown the ground beef. Remove meat from skillet, reserving 2 Tbsp of liquid. Add onions, garlic, baby carrots, and celery root; cook until lightly browned. Return ground beef to skillet; add rosemary, thyme, and brown sauce; bring to a simmer.

3. Fill individual baking dishes or crocks with the ground beef mixture. Top with mashed potatoes and bake for 35–45 minutes or until liquid is slightly bubbling around the sides. Serve immediately.

Exchanges/Choices
1 1/2 Starch
2 Lean Meat
1/2 Fat

Basic Nutritional Values
Calories 225
  Calories from Fat 65
Total Fat 7 g
  Saturated Fat 3 g
  Trans Fat 0.3 g
Cholesterol 40 mg
Sodium 395 mg
Total Carbohydrate 25 g
  Dietary Fiber 3 g
  Sugars 5 g
Protein 16 g

SAUTÉED CHICKEN PROVENÇAL

SERVES 4
SERVING SIZE: 1 BREAST

Exchanges/Choices
2 Vegetable
3 Lean Meat
3 Fat

Basic Nutritional Values
Calories 320
  Calories from Fat 160
Total Fat 18 g
  Saturated Fat 2.8 g
  Trans Fat 0 g
Cholesterol 65 mg
Sodium 245 mg
Total Carbohydrate 12 g
  Dietary Fiber 2 g
  Sugars 4 g
Protein 27 g

4	SKINLESS CHICKEN BREAST HALVES (4 OZ EACH)
	PINCH SALT
	BLACK PEPPER, TO TASTE
2	TBSP FLOUR
2 OZ + 2	TBSP OLIVE OIL
2	CLOVES GARLIC PUREE
1/2	CUP WHITE WINE
1	20-OZ CAN DICED TOMATOES
1	5-OZ CAN ARTICHOKE HEARTS, DRAINED AND QUARTERED
1/4	CUP OLIVES, COARSELY CHOPPED
2	TBSP BASIL, CHIFFONADE
1	TBSP MINCED PARSLEY
	PINCH SALT
1/2	CUP CHICKEN STOCK (SEE RECIPE ON P. 24)

1. Season the chicken breasts with salt and pepper and then coat with flour.

2. Preheat a sauté pan and add 2 oz olive oil. Sauté the breasts until golden brown on both sides. Transfer to a baking sheet and bake at 375°F until chicken reaches an internal temperature of 160°F, about 15–20 minutes.

3. While chicken is cooking, pour off oil and wipe clean. Heat pan over medium heat; add 2 Tbsp olive oil and the garlic puree. Sweat until the garlic turns white.

4. Deglaze with white wine and then add diced tomatoes; bring to a simmer over low heat. Cook tomatoes for 10–15 minutes. Add artichokes, olives, basil, parsley, salt, and chicken stock and bring to a simmer. Once simmering, add chicken breast and simmer for 10 minutes more. Serve immediately.

CHICKEN CASSOULET

2	TBSP PAPRIKA
1	TSP CHILI POWDER
1	TBSP MINCED GARLIC
1	TSP BLACK PEPPER
1	BUNCH FRESH THYME
2	TSP FRESH LEMON ZEST
4	SKINLESS CHICKEN THIGHS
4	SKINLESS CHICKEN DRUMSTICKS
1	TBSP EXTRA-VIRGIN OLIVE OIL
1	CUP WHITE WINE
1	QUART CHICKEN STOCK (SEE RECIPE ON P. 24)
2	CUPS COOKED WHITE BEANS
1	BUNCH FRESH THYME
1	CUP BABY CARROTS, MEDIUM DICE
1/2	CUP FRESH, WHOLE SHALLOTS, PEELED
1	CUP CELERY, MEDIUM DICE

SERVES 4
SERVING SIZE: 1/4 RECIPE

1. Combine paprika, chili powder, garlic, black pepper, thyme, and lemon zest. Rub mixture over chicken pieces, making sure that each is entirely covered. Lay chicken pieces flat onto a cookie sheet or sheet pan. (Make sure your pan has edges, so the juices don't run over.) Place a second sheet or pan over the chicken and weigh it down to press the chicken flat (you'll need something that weighs about 10 lbs). Place in the refrigerator and let sit 24 hours.

2. Preheat a large skillet and heat olive oil. Over medium-high heat, sear all sides of the meat. Deglaze with white wine and reduce liquid by half. Place meat and wine reduction in an oven-safe dish and add the chicken stock, white beans, thyme, carrots, shallots, and celery.

3. Cover dish and place in a preheated 250°F oven. Bake for 2–3 hours. Make sure the dish does not dry out; add more chicken stock if needed. Serve immediately.

Exchanges/Choices

1 1/2 Starch
2 Vegetable
4 Lean Meat
1 Fat

Basic Nutritional Values

Calories 385
  Calories from Fat 110
Total Fat 12 g
  Saturated Fat 2.7 g
  Trans Fat 0 g
Cholesterol 85 mg
Sodium 155 mg
Total Carbohydrate 35 g
  Dietary Fiber 9 g
  Sugars 6 g
Protein 5 g

Tips for the Kitchen

For easier preparation, you can follow the same steps using a crock pot or large 6-quart cast-iron pot with cover and still get great results.

SAFFRON RISOTTO

SERVES 4
SERVING SIZE: 1/4 RECIPE

	PINCH SAFFRON
1	TBSP OLIVE OIL
1/4	CUP MINCED ONIONS
1	CUP ARBORIO RICE
3	CUPS CHICKEN STOCK (SEE RECIPE ON P. 24)
1	TBSP BUTTER
1	TSP SALT
1/2	TSP WHITE PEPPER

Exchanges/Choices
2 Starch
1 Fat

Basic Nutritional Values
Calories 215
  Calories from Fat 65
Total Fat 7 g
  Saturated Fat 2.5 g
  Trans Fat 0 g
Cholesterol 10 mg
Sodium 610 mg
Total Carbohydrate 34 g
  Dietary Fiber 1 g
  Sugars 1 g
Protein 4 g

This recipe is
high in sodium.

1. In a small container, combine saffron and 2 Tbsp of warm water. Let steep until needed.

2. In a medium pot, heat the olive oil and add onion. Stir quickly to sauté. Add rice and 1 cup chicken stock. Bring to a simmer; then lower heat and continue at a low simmer. Add steeped saffron and continue to stir. Be sure to run the spoon along the bottom of the pan; this prevents the rice from burning and sticking to the pan.

3. As liquid is absorbed, add 1 cup of chicken stock to keep mixture wet. When this stock is absorbed, add the last cup of stock and butter, stirring to incorporate. Risotto is done when the rice is fully cooked and is tender but still retains its shape. Season with salt and pepper and serve.

LIMA BEANS WITH THYME

2 TSP OLIVE OIL

1/4 CUP DICED ONIONS

2 CUPS CHICKEN STOCK (SEE RECIPE ON P. 24)

1 LB LIMA BEANS

PINCH BLACK PEPPER

2 TSP MINCED THYME

SERVES 6
SERVING SIZE: 1/6 RECIPE

1. Preheat a pot over medium heat. Add olive oil and then the onions. Sweat onions until they are translucent.

2. Add the chicken stock, lima beans, and black pepper. Bring to a simmer. Continue cooking until lima beans are tender, about 20–25 minutes. Toss beans with fresh thyme; serve immediately.

Exchanges/Choices
2 Starch
2 Lean Meat

Basic Nutritional Values
Calories 235
  Calories from Fat 20
Total Fat 2.5 g
  Saturated Fat 0.4 g
  Trans Fat 0 g
Cholesterol 0 mg
Sodium 10 mg
Total Carbohydrate 40 g
  Dietary Fiber 13 g
  Sugars 6 g
Protein 15 g

sides

ROASTED CELERY ROOT AND BABY CARROTS

SERVES 8
SERVING SIZE: 1/8 RECIPE

Exchanges/Choices
2 Vegetable
1/2 Fat

Basic Nutritional Values
Calories 65
  Calories from Fat 30
Total Fat 3.5 g
  Saturated Fat 0.5 g
  Trans Fat 0 g
Cholesterol 0 mg
Sodium 365 mg
Total Carbohydrate 8 g
  Dietary Fiber 2 g
  Sugars 2 g
Protein 1 g

1 WHOLE (1 LB) CELERY ROOT, PEELED AND DICED
   INTO 1-INCH CUBES
2 TBSP OLIVE OIL
1 TSP SALT
   PINCH BLACK PEPPER
2 SPRIGS FRESH ROSEMARY, ABOUT 1 INCH LONG
1/2 LB BABY CARROTS

1. Place diced celery root in a medium bowl. Add 1 Tbsp olive oil, 1/2 tsp salt, black pepper, and fresh rosemary; toss until fully coated. Place in a baking dish and bake at 375°F for about 45 minutes or until golden brown.

2. Place the carrots in a medium bowl. Add 1 Tbsp olive oil, 1/2 tsp salt, and black pepper; toss until fully coated. Place in a baking dish and bake at 375°F for about 30 minutes or until fully cooked. You can place carrots into oven 15 minutes after the celery root to ensure that they are finished and come out at the same time.

3. When both are done, combine in a serving bowl and serve hot.

Tips for the Kitchen

The trick to getting the best flavor from this recipe is to cook the vegetables separately, so they retain their true flavor.

Celery root is available throughout the year at most grocery stores. It is the size of a large grapefruit and has a rough outer skin that is pale to slightly green in color.

CHOCOLATE PUDDING WITH PISTACHIO CREAM

1   1.4-OZ BOX SUGAR-FREE INSTANT
      CHOCOLATE PUDDING
2   TBSP PISTACHIO NUTS, FINELY GROUND
1   CUP FAT-FREE WHIPPED TOPPING

SERVES 4
SERVING SIZE: 1/4 RECIPE

1. Prepare the pudding according to package directions. Cover and refrigerate until needed.

2. Fold the pistachio nuts into the whipped topping. Place a dollop of pistachio cream on the chocolate pudding and serve.

Exchanges/Choices
1 Carbohydrate

Basic Nutritional Values
Calories 90
  Calories from Fat 20
Total Fat 2 g
  Saturated Fat 0.2 g
  Trans Fat 0 g
Cholesterol 0 mg
Sodium 320 mg
Total Carbohydrate 15 g
  Dietary Fiber 1 g
  Sugars 2 g
Protein 2 g

BREAD PUDDING WITH CHOCOLATE AND ORANGE

SERVES 12
SERVING SIZE: 1/12 RECIPE

Exchanges/Choices
1 Carbohydrate
1/2 Fat

Basic Nutritional Values
Calories 90
  Calories from Fat 20
Total Fat 2.5 g
  Saturated Fat 1.4 g
  Trans Fat 0 g
Cholesterol 0 mg
Sodium 100 mg
Total Carbohydrate 13 g
  Dietary Fiber 1 g
  Sugars 9 g
Protein 4 g

COOKING SPRAY
2 CUPS STALE BREAD, CUT INTO BITE-SIZE PIECES
1/2 CUP SEMISWEET CHOCOLATE CHIPS
1 CUP LOW-FAT MILK
1 1/2 CUPS EGG SUBSTITUTE
1 TSP CINNAMON
1/4 CUP SUGAR
1 TBSP ORANGE ZEST

1. Prepare eight custard dishes and spray with nonstick cooking spray. Evenly distribute the stale bread and the chocolate chips into the custard cups.

2. Preheat the oven to 325°F.

3. Whisk together the milk, egg substitute, cinnamon, sugar, and orange zest to make custard. Pour custard mixture evenly into the custard dishes and arrange them in a large flat baking pan. Fill the pan with hot water, making sure that the water comes up to about three-quarters of each custard dish. Place baking pan in the oven. Cook until custard is set, about 45 minutes. Gently remove from water bath and serve warm.

PINEAPPLE TARTE TATIN

1 TBSP CANOLA OIL

1 TBSP SUGAR

1/4 TSP CINNAMON

2 CUPS PINEAPPLE, DRAINED, SMALL DICE

1 SHEET FROZEN PUFF PASTRY, THAWED

FAT-FREE WHIPPED TOPPING (OPTIONAL)

FRESH MINT (OPTIONAL)

SERVES 4
SERVING SIZE: 1/4 RECIPE

1. In a small pan, heat the oil; add sugar, cinnamon, and pineapple. Cook until the pineapple softens and the sugar begins to caramelize. Remove from heat and portion into 4 ramekins. Reserve any liquid that remains.

2. Cut the puff pastry into four rounds to fit the top of ramekin (each round should weigh about 1/2 oz). Place the pastry tops on the ramekins, pushing the pineapple mixture down. Make a small hole in the top of the pastry to let steam escape. Brush tops with leftover pineapple liquid.

3. Preheat oven to 375°F. Place the ramekins on a baking sheet and bake for 25–30 minutes or until pastry is golden brown. Allow the tarts to cool slightly.

4. Turn ramekins upside down and lightly tap to remove the tarts. Allow to cool a little more. If desired, garnish with a dollop of whipped topping and a sprig of fresh mint.

Exchanges/Choices
1 Carbohydrate
1 1/2 Fat

Basic Nutritional Values
Calories 140
Calories from Fat 65
Total Fat 7 g
Saturated Fat 1.3 g
Trans Fat 1.4 g
Cholesterol 0 mg
Sodium 70 mg
Total Carbohydrate 18 g
Dietary Fiber 2 g
Sugars 11 g
Protein 1 g

BANANA CREAM BITES

SERVES 12
SERVING SIZE: 2 BANANA BITES

12	OZ FAT-FREE CREAM CHEESE
1/4	CUP SUGAR
1	BANANA, MASHED
1/2	TSP VANILLA EXTRACT
1	CUP LIGHT WHIPPED TOPPING
24	MINI PHYLLO DOUGH SHELLS

Whisk together cream cheese, sugar, banana, vanilla, and light whipped topping. Place into a pastry bag with a star tip and distribute evenly into phyllo dough shells. Serve immediately.

Exchanges/Choices
1 Carbohydrate
1/2 Fat

Basic Nutritional Values
Calories 105
  Calories from Fat 20
Total Fat 2.5 g
  Saturated Fat 0.7 g
  Trans Fat 0 g
Cholesterol 5 mg
Sodium 225 mg
Total Carbohydrate 15 g
  Dietary Fiber 0 g
  Sugars 7 g
Protein 4 g

March
&
April

SEASONAL BOUNTY

THIS IS the time of year when the markets begin showing off their fresh vegetables. These displays reveal the freshness and quality that you'll find in the wide variety of fruits and vegetables available in spring and summer. Eating fresh fruits and vegetables offers a ton of health benefits, including adding important vitamins, minerals, antioxidants, and dietary fiber to our diets. The quality and freshness of these products directly relate to their health benefits. The older the product, the less flavor, texture, and nutritional quality it'll provide. So how do we identify fresh fruits and vegetables? Below are some simple tips that can help.

FINDING FRESHNESS

- Fruits and vegetables should look fresh. Colors should be bright, with little or no blemishes.
- Vegetables should be firm to the touch and not limp or dull.
- Leafy vegetables should be crisp and uniformly green in color. Look for vegetables that are not limp or irregular in shape or size.
- Both fruits and vegetables can feel slightly heavier than they appear, indicating that they have been freshly picked. Ones that are lighter in weight, wrinkled, or have a blotchy skin tone should be avoided.
- Mushrooms should be small to medium in size. Caps should be closed around the stem, whereas color should be uniform, from creamy white to brown.
- Onions should be firm, with no visible bruises or blemishes, and have no sprouting leaves.
- Tomatoes should be smooth, well ripened, and free of blemishes. If they include the vine, inspect it to see if it is green and fresh looking. Discolored and wrinkled vines indicate that the tomatoes may have been sitting too long.
- Fruits should be purchased in season and preferably locally grown.
- Purchase only as much as called for in the recipe. This allows you to enjoy your fruits at peak flavor and quality.
- Handle fruits and vegetables carefully, when both purchasing and storing them.

Resource: *www.ams.usda.gov/howtobuy/fveg.htm.*

SHRIMP-STUFFED MUSHROOMS

20	LARGE MUSHROOMS
1	TSP OLIVE OIL
1	CUP RAW SHRIMP, CHOPPED
2	TBSP ONIONS, SMALL DICE
1/4	CUP RED PEPPERS, SMALL DICE
1	LARGE EGG
1/4	CUP BREAD CRUMBS
1	TBSP CHOPPED CHIVES
1	TSP LEMON JUICE

SERVES 10
SERVING SIZE: 2 MUSHROOMS

Exchanges/Choices
1 Vegetable
1 Lean Meat

Basic Nutritional Values
Calories 55
  Calories from Fat 20
Total Fat 2 g
  Saturated Fat 0.4 g
  Trans Fat 0 g
Cholesterol 40 mg
Sodium 90 mg
Total Carbohydrate 4 g
  Dietary Fiber 1 g
  Sugars 1 g
Protein 6 g

1. Preheat oven to 375°F.

2. Remove stems from mushrooms and finely chop the mushroom stems. Set aside mushroom caps.

3. Preheat a sauté pan and add olive oil. Sauté shrimp until cooked, about 4 minutes. Remove shrimp from pan.

4. Add chopped mushroom stems, onions, and red peppers to the pan and stir until cooked; remove from heat.

5. Place shrimp and vegetable mixture in a food processor and chop. Transfer mixture to a bowl and fold in the egg, bread crumbs, chives, and lemon juice. Evenly scoop shrimp mixture into mushroom caps.

6. Arrange stuffed mushroom caps in a baking dish. Bake for 25–30 minutes. Serve hot.

MINI HAM AND CHEESE QUICHE BITES

SERVES 4
SERVING SIZE: 1/4 RECIPE

Exchanges/Choices
1/2 Starch
1 Lean Meat
1 Fat

Basic Nutritional Values
Calories 125
  Calories from Fat 55
Total Fat 6 g
  Saturated Fat 1.4 g
  Trans Fat 0 g
Cholesterol 15 mg
Sodium 410 mg
Total Carbohydrate 7 g
  Dietary Fiber 0 g
  Sugars 0 g
Protein 10 g

3/4   CUP EGG SUBSTITUTE
  3   OZ LOW-FAT LEAN HAM, DICED
  3   TBSP CHEDDAR CHEESE, GRATED
  1   TBSP MINCED FRESH CHIVES
 12   MINI PHYLLO DOUGH SHELLS

1. In a medium bowl, whisk together the egg substitute, ham, cheese, and chives. Carefully pour the egg mixture into the phyllo shells.

2. Place the filled shells in the oven and bake at 375°F for 12–15 minutes or until the egg mixture is fully cooked. Remove the shells from the oven and let rest for 2 minutes before serving.

CHICKEN AND RICE SOUP

1	TBSP OLIVE OIL
1/2	CUP ONIONS, SMALL DICE
1/2	CUP CELERY, SMALL DICE
1/2	CUP CARROTS, SMALL DICE
1	CUP COOKED CHICKEN, DICED
1	CUP COOKED BROWN RICE
1	QUART FORTIFIED CHICKEN STOCK (SEE RECIPE ON P. 24)
1	TBSP MINCED PARSLEY

Preheat a large pot and heat olive oil. Add onions, celery, and carrots and sweat them. Add chicken, brown rice, and chicken stock; bring to a simmer. Just before serving, garnish with parsley.

SERVES 6
SERVING SIZE: 1/6 RECIPE

Exchanges/Choices
1/2 Starch
1 Vegetable
1 Lean Meat
1/2 Fat

Basic Nutritional Values
Calories 130
  Calories from Fat 45
Total Fat 5 g
  Saturated Fat 1 g
  Trans Fat 0 g
Cholesterol 30 mg
Sodium 55 mg
Total Carbohydrate 11 g
  Dietary Fiber 1 g
  Sugars 1 g
Protein 11 g

starters

CREAM OF BROCCOLI SOUP

SERVES 8
SERVING SIZE: 1/8 RECIPE

Exchanges/Choices
1 Carbohydrate
1 Fat
Basic Nutritional Values
Calories 110
Calories from Fat 55
Total Fat 6 g
Saturated Fat 1 g
Trans Fat 0 g
Cholesterol 5 mg
Sodium 350 mg
Total Carbohydrate 11 g
Dietary Fiber 2 g
Sugars 3 g
Protein 4 g

1 1/2	LB BROCCOLI, CHOPPED
6	CUPS CHICKEN STOCK (SEE RECIPE ON P. 24)
3	TBSP OLIVE OIL
1	CUP ONIONS, SMALL DICE
1/4	CUP WHOLE-WHEAT FLOUR
1	CUP FAT-FREE HALF & HALF
1	TSP SALT
1	TSP WHITE PEPPER

1. Wash the broccoli thoroughly. Using a vegetable peeler, remove the tough outer layer from the broccoli stalks. Chop broccoli and set aside 1 cup of florets for garnish.

2. Bring chicken stock to a simmer and add chopped broccoli. Cook for a few minutes or until broccoli is tender, making sure the color does not become dull.

3. Puree cooked broccoli and 1 cup of chicken stock in a food processor. Set aside.

4. Add olive oil and onions to a pot and gently cook. Sprinkle flour and stir to mix. On low heat, continue cooking, making sure flour is absorbed and slightly turns color. Slowly whisk hot chicken stock into flour mixture and bring to a simmer. Add broccoli puree and half & half; bring to a simmer, stirring to combine ingredients. Season with salt and pepper and garnish with florets. Serve hot.

Chicken and Vegetable Soup with Avocado

1	TBSP OLIVE OIL
1	CUP ONIONS, MEDIUM DICE
1/2	CUP CELERY, SMALL DICE
1/2	CUP CARROTS, SMALL DICE
1/2	CUP RED PEPPERS, JULIENNED
1	CUP COOKED, DICED CHICKEN
1	QUART FORTIFIED CHICKEN STOCK (SEE RECIPE ON P. 24)
1/2	CUP MINCED SCALLIONS
1	AVOCADO, SLICED

SERVES 6
SERVING SIZE: 1/6 RECIPE

Preheat a large pot; add and heat olive oil. Add onions, celery, carrots, and red peppers and sweat them. Add chicken and chicken stock; bring to a simmer. Add scallions. Ladle into soup bowls. Top with sliced avocado and serve.

Exchanges/Choices
1 Vegetable
1 Lean Meat
1 1/2 Fat

Basic Nutritional Values
Calories 145
  Calories from Fat 70
Total Fat 8 g
  Saturated Fat 1.5 g
  Trans Fat 0 g
Cholesterol 30 mg
Sodium 55 mg
Total Carbohydrate 8 g
  Dietary Fiber 3 g
  Sugars 3 g
Protein 11 g

CURRY CHICKEN SOUP WITH MINT YOGURT

SERVES 8
SERVING SIZE: 1/8 RECIPE

8	OZ RAW CHICKEN, WHITE MEAT, SMALL DICE
2	TBSP CURRY
2	TBSP OLIVE OIL
1/2	CUP WHITE ONIONS, SMALL DICE
1/4	CUP CELERY, SMALL DICE
1/4	CUP CARROTS, SMALL DICE
1/2	CUP RED PEPPERS, SMALL DICE
2	MEDIUM POTATOES, PEELED AND MEDIUM DICE
1	QUART HOT CHICKEN STOCK (SEE RECIPE ON P. 24)
1/2	CUP PEELED GRANNY SMITH APPLES, SMALL DICE
1	TBSP LEMON JUICE
1/2	CUP PLAIN YOGURT
10	FRESH MINT LEAVES, CHIFFONADE

1. In a clean bowl, combine the chicken and curry until fully coated. Refrigerate overnight.

2. Add 1 Tbsp olive oil to a preheated medium pot. Add chicken and sauté until cooked, about 8–10 minutes. Remove chicken and set aside.

3. Add 1 Tbsp of olive oil to pan again; add white onions, celery, carrots, and red peppers; sauté until vegetables are cooked but not browned, stirring often. Add diced potatoes and hot chicken stock; bring to a simmer. Cover and simmer on low heat until potatoes are very tender. When potatoes are tender, remove from heat and allow to cool.

4. When potatoes have cooled enough to safely handle, puree them in a food processor or blender.

5. Place puree back on the stove and bring to a low simmer. Add cooked diced chicken and continue to simmer until it reaches an internal temperature of 160°F.

6. In a separate bowl, toss apples with lemon juice and set aside until needed.

7. Place soup into serving bowls. Garnish with a fresh dollop of yogurt, diced apples, and mint leaves. Serve immediately.

Exchanges/Choices
1 Carbohydrate
1 Lean Meat
1/2 Fat

Basic Nutritional Values
Calories 120
  Calories from Fat 45
Total Fat 5 g
  Saturated Fat 1.1 g
  Trans Fat 0 g
Cholesterol 20 mg
Sodium 35 mg
Total Carbohydrate 11 g
  Dietary Fiber 2 g
  Sugars 3 g
Protein 8 g

GRILLED LAMB CHOPS

SERVES 4
SERVING SIZE: 1 LAMB PIECE

2 FRENCHED LAMB RACKS, ABOUT 1 1/2 LB, TRIMMED OF FAT
1 TBSP OLIVE OIL
1 TBSP MINCED GARLIC
1/2 TSP SALT
    PINCH FRESH GROUND PEPPER
2 SPRIGS FRESH ROSEMARY (ABOUT 1 INCH EACH)

Exchanges/Choices
3 Lean Meat
1 Fat
Basic Nutritional Values
Calories 190
Calories from Fat 90
Total Fat 10 g
Saturated Fat 3 g
Trans Fat 0 g
Cholesterol 70 mg
Sodium 350 mg
Total Carbohydrate 1 g
Dietary Fiber 0 g
Sugars 0 g
Protein 22 g

1. Cut each lamb rack into four pieces with two bones, leaving one bone with an equal amount of meat.

2. Combine olive oil, garlic, salt, pepper, and rosemary. Fully coat lamb ribs and marinate for 2 hours in the refrigerator.

3. Preheat your grill and cook the chops over even heat. Flip chops over to cook both sides. Use a meat thermometer to check when the racks are done.

Tips for the Kitchen

These are the temperatures for doneness for lamb chops.

Medium rare: 145°F
Medium: 160°F
Well done: 170°F

Cajun Lemon Shrimp

1   LB FRESH SHRIMP, CLEANED
2   TSP CRUSHED OREGANO
1 1/2   TSP FRESH THYME
2   TSP PAPRIKA
1/2   TSP CAYENNE PEPPER
1   Tbsp OLIVE OIL
    Dash BLACK PEPPER
    Juice AND ZEST OF 1 LEMON

SERVES 4
SERVING SIZE: 1/4 RECIPE

1. Combine all ingredients (except lemon juice and zest) and marinate for 1 hour in the refrigerator.

2. In a preheated sauté pan, quickly cook shrimp. Deglaze with lemon juice and toss, coating shrimp in the sauce. Serve immediately.

Exchanges/Choices
2 Lean Meat

Basic Nutritional Values
Calories 105
  Calories from Fat 40
Total Fat 4.5 g
  Saturated Fat 0.7 g
  Trans Fat 0 g
Cholesterol 130 mg
Sodium 155 mg
Total Carbohydrate 2 g
  Dietary Fiber 0 g
  Sugars 1 g
Protein 14 g

MINI TURKEY MEATBALLS

SERVES 6
SERVING SIZE: 1/6 RECIPE

1	LB GROUND TURKEY BREAST
2	LARGE EGGS
1/2	CUP BREAD CRUMBS
1/4	CUP GRATED PARMESAN CHEESE
1/4	CUP ONIONS, FINELY DICED
1	TBSP MINCED PARSLEY
1/2	TSP BLACK PEPPER
	COOKING SPRAY

Combine all ingredients and mix by hand. Do not overmix. Shape into small fork-size balls. Heat a skillet and spray with cooking spray. Cook mini meatballs until browned and done (an internal temperature of 160°F).

Exchanges/Choices
1/2 Starch
2 Lean Meat

Basic Nutritional Values
Calories 140
  Calories from Fat 30
Total Fat 3.5 g
  Saturated Fat 1.4 g
  Trans Fat 0 g
Cholesterol 110 mg
Sodium 140 mg
Total Carbohydrate 8 g
  Dietary Fiber 1 g
  Sugars 1 g
Protein 18 g

STEAK AU POIVRE

4   BEEF TENDERLOINS (4 OZ EACH)
1   TBSP CRUSHED PEPPERCORNS
1   TBSP OLIVE OIL
1/4   CUP COGNAC
1/2   CUP BROWN SAUCE (SEE RECIPE ON P. 22)

SERVES 4
SERVING SIZE: 1 STEAK

1. Evenly coat beef with peppercorns.

2. Heat pan and add olive oil. Sear meat on both sides until golden brown. Add cognac and allow to flame. (Be sure to use caution when the cognac ignites. Work in a space with lots of ventilation.) Reduce liquid by half, add brown sauce, and simmer, coating both sides of beef. Serve immediately.

Exchanges/Choices
3 Lean Meat
1 Fat

Basic Nutritional Values
Calories 205
  Calories from Fat 80
Total Fat 9 g
  Saturated Fat 2.7 g
  Trans Fat 0 g
Cholesterol 60 mg
Sodium 50 mg
Total Carbohydrate 4 g
  Dietary Fiber 1 g
  Sugars 0 g
Protein 22 g

WHOLE-WHEAT CAPELLINI WITH VEGETABLES

SERVES 4
SERVING SIZE: 1/4 RECIPE

Exchanges/Choices

3 Starch
1 Vegetable
1 Fat

Basic Nutritional Values

Calories 310
  Calories from Fat 45
Total Fat 5 g
  Saturated Fat 0.7 g
  Trans Fat 0 g
Cholesterol 5 mg
Sodium 30 mg
Total Carbohydrate 52 g
  Dietary Fiber 7 g
  Sugars 5 g
Protein 13 g

1	LARGE CARROT, PEELED
1/2	LB WHOLE-WHEAT CAPELLINI (ALSO CALLED ANGEL HAIR PASTA)
2	TSP OLIVE OIL
1	CLOVE GARLIC, MINCED
2	TSP MINCED GINGER
1/2	LB SHIITAKE MUSHROOMS
1/2	CUP WHITE WINE
6	OZ EDAMAME (BOILED GREEN SOYBEANS), SHUCKED
1/2	LB GREEN BEANS, STEMS REMOVED
12	OZ FORTIFIED CHICKEN STOCK (SEE RECIPE ON P. 24)
2	TBSP FRESH BASIL, CHIFFONADE

1. Peel carrot and discard skins. Using a peeler, cut carrot into long, wide ribbon cuts.

2. Bring water to a boil and cook pasta until desired doneness. Drain and cool.

3. Preheat a large skillet and add olive oil. Add garlic and ginger; sweat for a few seconds. Add shiitake mushrooms and wine; cook until tender. Add carrot ribbons, edamame beans, green beans, and fortified chicken stock. Simmer until carrot ribbons are firm but cooked, about 5–10 minutes.

4. Portion pasta into individual bowls. Add vegetables and broth to each bowl and garnish with fresh basil. Serve hot.

BAKED SALMON WITH MANGO VINAIGRETTE

4   SALMON STEAKS/FILLETS (6 OZ EACH)
2   TSP EXTRA-VIRGIN OLIVE OIL
    PINCH SALT
    GREEN PEPPERCORNS, TO TASTE
8   SPRIGS FRESH THYME
4   TBSP MANGO VINAIGRETTE (SEE RECIPE
    ON P. 30)

SERVES 4
SERVING SIZE: 1 FILLET

1. Place salmon in a baking dish. Using a pastry brush, lightly coat salmon with extra-virgin olive oil. Season with salt and green peppercorns; place a few sprigs of thyme on top of the salmon. Bake for 15–20 minutes at 375°F until salmon is fully cooked.

2. Drizzle 1 Tbsp of mango vinaigrette over the salmon and serve immediately.

Exchanges/Choices
5 Lean Meat
2 Fat

Basic Nutritional Values
Calories 325
Calories from Fat 170
Total Fat 19 g
Saturated Fat 3 g
Trans Fat 0 g
Cholesterol 115 mg
Sodium 90 mg
Total Carbohydrate 1 g
Dietary Fiber 0 g
Sugars 1 g
Protein 36 g

FLANK STEAK DIANE

SERVES 4
SERVING SIZE: 1/4 RECIPE

12 TBSP OLIVE OIL

3 CLOVES GARLIC, MINCED

1 LB FLANK STEAK

1 TBSP WORCESTERSHIRE SAUCE

JUICE AND ZEST OF 1 LEMON

Exchanges/Choices
3 Lean Meat
2 1/2 Fat

Basic Nutritional Values
Calories 245
 Calories from Fat 145
Total Fat 16 g
 Saturated Fat 3.8 g
 Trans Fat 0 g
Cholesterol 40 mg
Sodium 100 mg
Total Carbohydrate 2 g
 Dietary Fiber 0 g
 Sugars 1 g
Protein 22 g

1. Combine the olive oil and garlic; marinate flank steak for 2 hours.

2. Heat a skillet over medium-high heat and sear meat until golden brown. Turn and brown other side. Once both sides are browned, remove from heat and place in a baking dish. Season beef with Worcestershire sauce, lemon zest, and lemon juice. Bake at 400°F until done as desired. Serve immediately.

CHICKEN STIR-FRY

Marinade

1 TBSP MINCED GINGER

1 TBSP MINCED GARLIC

2 TBSP SCALLIONS, DICED

1 TBSP SESAME OIL

1 LB BONELESS, SKINLESS CHICKEN, CUT INTO THIN STRIPS

2 TBSP CANOLA OIL

1 CUP SHIITAKE MUSHROOMS, STEMS REMOVED

2 TBSP SCALLIONS, DICED

1/2 CUP RED ONIONS, SLICED THIN

2 HEADS BABY BOK CHOY, THINLY SLICED

1 CUP BROCCOLI FLORETS

1/2 CUP GRATED CARROTS

1/4 CUP HOISIN SAUCE

1/2 CUP FORTIFIED CHICKEN STOCK (SEE RECIPE ON P. 24)

2 CUPS COOKED RICE

Exchanges/Choices
1 1/2 Starch
2 Vegetable
3 Lean Meat
2 1/2 Fat

Basic Nutritional Values
Calories 405
Calories from Fat 155
Total Fat 17 g
Saturated Fat 2.8 g
Trans Fat 0 g
Cholesterol 70 mg
Sodium 320 mg
Total Carbohydrate 35 g
Dietary Fiber 3 g
Sugars 8 g
Protein 28 g

1. Combine marinade ingredients and add chicken. Refrigerate for 30 minutes.

2. Heat a large pot. Heat 1 Tbsp canola oil and then add half of the marinated chicken mixture, stirring quickly. Once chicken is cooked, remove from pot and repeat with remaining chicken mixture (do not add more oil). When that mixture is done, remove from heat and set aside.

3. Slice shiitake mushrooms in half. Add remaining canola oil to pot; add scallions and red onions. Stir to cook. Add bok choy and broccoli and continue to cook. Add shiitake mushrooms and grated carrots; continue to stir quickly.

4. Add the cooked chicken and any juice, hoisin sauce, and chicken stock. Bring to a simmer, being sure to coat all of the meat and vegetables. Serve over cooked rice.

CREAMY POLENTA

SERVES 8
SERVING SIZE: 1/8 RECIPE

1	QUART CHICKEN STOCK (SEE RECIPE ON P. 24)
1	CUP CORNMEAL, YELLOW OR WHITE
1/4	CUP PARMESAN CHEESE
	PINCH WHITE PEPPER

Bring chicken stock to a simmer. In a slow, steady stream, add cornmeal while stirring to incorporate. Reduce heat to low and allow mixture to simmer, stirring often. Continue to cook for 25–30 minutes or until polenta is fully cooked and creamy in texture. Add additional chicken stock to reach desired consistency. Stir in Parmesan cheese and white pepper; serve warm.

Exchanges/Choices
1 Starch

Basic Nutritional Values
Calories 80
  Calories from Fat 15
Total Fat 1.5 g
  Saturated Fat 0.6 g
  Trans Fat 0 g
Cholesterol 5 mg
Sodium 30 mg
Total Carbohydrate 14 g
  Dietary Fiber 1 g
  Sugars 0 g
Protein 3 g

Top left: Blueberry Yogurt Smoothie, p. 37
Right: Crunchy Peach Smoothie, p. 36
Bottom: Strawberry Smoothie, p. 35

Spinach, Tomato, and Feta Cheese Baked Egg, p. 42

Omelet with Cheddar and Low-Fat Ham, p. 40

Chicken Tortellini Soup, p. 57
Turkey and Swiss Wrap, p. 50

Grilled Lamb Chops, p. 82
Simple Grilled Asparagus, p. 93

Flank Steak Diane, p. 88
Spinach Salad with Tangerines, Onions, and Walnuts, p. 104

Sautéed Chicken Provençal, p. 64

Spinach Strudel, p. 55

ROASTED CARROTS AND PARSNIPS WITH GARLIC AND THYME

1 CUP PARSNIPS, PEELED AND DICED

1 CUP CARROTS, PEELED AND DICED

2 CLOVES GARLIC, MINCED

2 TBSP OLIVE OIL

1 TSP SALT

PINCH BLACK PEPPER

2 TSP MINCED FRESH THYME

SERVES 4
SERVING SIZE: 1/4 RECIPE

Peel the parsnips and carrots and cut into medium chunks. Add to a large bowl. Add remaining ingredients and toss to combine. Place on a baking sheet and roast at 375°F for 45 minutes or until fully roasted. While roasting, be sure to check that the vegetables are browning evenly. Serve immediately.

Exchanges/Choices

2 Vegetable

1 Fat

Basic Nutritional Values

Calories 105

　Calories from Fat 65

Total Fat 7 g

　Saturated Fat 0.9 g

　Trans Fat 0 g

Cholesterol 0 mg

Sodium 605 mg

Total Carbohydrate 10 g

　Dietary Fiber 3 g

　Sugars 3 g

Protein 1 g

This recipe is high in sodium.

SPINACH, TOMATO, AND ROASTED GARLIC POLENTA

SERVES 8
SERVING SIZE: 1/8 RECIPE

Exchanges/Choices
1 Starch

Basic Nutritional Values
Calories 95
  Calories from Fat 20
Total Fat 2.5 g
  Saturated Fat 1 g
  Trans Fat 0 g
Cholesterol 5 mg
Sodium 80 mg
Total Carbohydrate 15 g
  Dietary Fiber 2 g
  Sugars 1 g
Protein 4 g

1	QUART CHICKEN STOCK (SEE RECIPE ON P. 24)
1	CUP CORNMEAL, YELLOW OR WHITE
1/4	CUP PARMESAN CHEESE
	PINCH WHITE PEPPER
1	TSP OLIVE OIL
2	CUPS FRESH SPINACH, CHOPPED
1	CUP TOMATO, SMALL DICE
1	TBSP ROASTED GARLIC, MINCED (SEE RECIPE ON P. 28)

1. Bring chicken stock to a simmer. In a slow, steady stream, add cornmeal and stir to incorporate. Reduce heat to low and allow to simmer, stirring often. Continue to cook for 25–30 minutes or until polenta is fully cooked and creamy in texture. If needed, add more chicken stock to adjust consistency. Stir in Parmesan cheese and add white pepper to taste.

2. In a separate pan, heat 1 tsp olive oil. Sauté spinach until just wilted; reserve.

3. Fold the sautéed spinach, tomato, and roasted garlic into the polenta mixture. Serve immediately.

SIMPLE GRILLED ASPARAGUS

COOKING SPRAY

1 LB ASPARAGUS, BOTTOMS REMOVED

1 TBSP EXTRA-VIRGIN OLIVE OIL

PINCH SALT

PEPPER, TO TASTE

JUICE OF 1 LEMON

SERVES 4
SERVING SIZE: 1/4 RECIPE

1. Preheat grill to medium. Coat the grate with cooking spray so food does not stick to the surface.

2. Gently toss asparagus with olive oil, salt, and pepper. Place on grill and cook until asparagus has grill marks, about 1–2 minutes. Roll asparagus over to grill the other side. Remove from the grill and chill in the refrigerator. Splash with fresh lemon juice before serving. Serve chilled.

Exchanges/Choices

1 Vegetable

1/2 Fat

Basic Nutritional Values

Calories 50

  Calories from Fat 30

Total Fat 3.5 g

  Saturated Fat 0.5 g

  Trans Fat 0 g

Cholesterol 0 mg

Sodium 10 mg

Total Carbohydrate 4 g

  Dietary Fiber 1 g

  Sugars 2 g

Protein 2 g

SOUTHERN-STYLE KALE

SERVES 4
SERVING SIZE: 1/4 RECIPE

2	LB KALE
3	QUARTS WATER
1	TBSP SALT
1	TBSP OLIVE OIL
1/2	CUP DICED ONIONS
1/4	CUP HAM, SMALL DICE
1	CUP FORTIFIED CHICKEN STOCK (SEE RECIPE ON P. 24)
	FRESH GROUND PEPPER, TO TASTE

Exchanges/Choices
2 Vegetable
1 Fat

Basic Nutritional Values
Calories 100
 Calories from Fat 40
Total Fat 4.5 g
 Saturated Fat 0.7 g
 Trans Fat 0 g
Cholesterol 5 mg
Sodium 450 mg
Total Carbohydrate 11 g
 Dietary Fiber 4 g
 Sugars 3 g
Protein 6 g

1. Clean kale by removing leaves from stems. Coarsely chop the leaves and discard stems. Thoroughly wash leaves and drain to remove any dirt.

2. In a large pot, bring water to a boil and add salt. Add kale and simmer for about 3–5 minutes, until leaves become tender. Drain water and remove kale.

3. Add olive oil to the pot and sweat the onions. Add ham and continue to cook. Add kale and sauté. Add chicken stock. Cook until kale is very tender; season with pepper. Serve immediately.

POTATO PANCAKES

1 LB YUKON GOLD POTATOES, GRATED

1/2 CUP DICED ONIONS

1 LARGE EGG

2 TBSP MATZO MEAL

1 TSP SALT

1 TSP PEPPER

1 TSP GARLIC POWDER

COOKING SPRAY

SERVES 4
SERVING SIZE: 1/4 RECIPE

1. Preheat the oven to 375°F. Using the grater attachment on a food processor or a box grater, grate the potatoes and place them in a medium bowl.

2. Add the remaining ingredients (except cooking spray) and combine well. (The potatoes may turn slightly brown, but this will disappear during cooking.)

3. Heat a large nonstick skillet over medium heat. Spray the skillet with cooking spray.

4. In 1/4-cup batches, place mixture in the skillet, making sure each potato pancake is evenly spaced. Cook the pancakes on each side until golden brown in color.

5. Transfer the potato pancakes to a baking sheet and place in the oven for 20 minutes or until fully cooked inside and out.

6. Serve immediately with a side of unsweetened applesauce or fat-free sour cream (not included in nutritional analysis).

Exchanges/Choices
2 Starch

Basic Nutritional Values
Calories 165
  Calories from Fat 15
Total Fat 1.5 g
  Saturated Fat 0.4 g
  Trans Fat 0 g
Cholesterol 55 mg
Sodium 610 mg
Total Carbohydrate 34 g
  Dietary Fiber 3 g
  Sugars 3 g
Protein 5 g

This recipe is
high in sodium.

BRAISED ARTICHOKES WITH WINE, GARLIC, AND OLIVE OIL

SERVES 4
SERVING SIZE: 2 ARTICHOKES

8	MEDIUM ARTICHOKES
3	CUPS WHITE WINE
1	CUP OLIVE OIL
6	CLOVES GARLIC
8–10	SPRIGS FRESH THYME
1	LEMON, HALVED AND SEEDS REMOVED
1/2	TSP SALT

Exchanges/Choices
----
3 Vegetable
1 Fat

Basic Nutritional Values

Calories 135
 Calories from Fat 35
Total Fat 4 g
 Saturated Fat 0.6 g
 Trans Fat 0 g
Cholesterol 0 mg
Sodium 170 mg
Total Carbohydrate 22 g
 Dietary Fiber 16 g
 Sugars 2 g
Protein 5 g

1. Cut off the fibrous part of stem and discard. Remove and discard the darker and toughest leaves. Using a sharp knife, trim away the tops of the leaves. Scoop out inside purple leaves and hairs with a small spoon. To prevent discoloration, store artichokes in water with a little lemon juice until needed.

2. Place artichokes in a pot large enough that they fit snug. Combine white wine, olive oil, garlic, thyme, lemon, and salt; bring to a simmer. Liquid should cover about 3/4 of the artichokes. Cook covered at low heat for about 30 minutes or until artichokes are tender.

EXTRA-THICK LEMON YOGURT

32 OZ LOW-FAT VANILLA YOGURT

1 TSP LEMON ZEST, SOME RESERVED FOR GARNISH

1 TSP FRESH LEMON JUICE

SERVES 32
SERVING SIZE: 1 TBSP

1. Drape two large pieces of cheesecloth over a medium bowl. Place yogurt on center of cloth; bring corners together and tie, so yogurt can hang without the cloth opening up. Hang yogurt in the refrigerator overnight with a bowl underneath to capture liquid.

2. Remove thickened yogurt from cheesecloth and place in a large bowl. Fold in lemon zest and fresh lemon juice. Serve chilled.

Exchanges/Choices
Free Food

Basic Nutritional Values
Calories 10
  Calories from Fat 0
Total Fat 0 g
  Saturated Fat 0.1 g
  Trans Fat 0 g
Cholesterol 0 mg
Sodium 0 mg
Total Carbohydrate 2 g
  Dietary Fiber 0 g
  Sugars 2 g
Protein 1 g

SIMPLE BREAD PUDDING

SERVES 8
SERVING SIZE: 1 DISH

Exchanges/Choices
2 Carbohydrate

Basic Nutritional Values
Calories 160
  Calories from Fat 30
Total Fat 3.5 g
  Saturated Fat 1.1 g
  Trans Fat 0 g
Cholesterol 110 mg
Sodium 115 mg
Total Carbohydrate 27 g
  Dietary Fiber 2 g
  Sugars 18 g
Protein 6 g

COOKING SPRAY

2	CUPS STALE BREAD, CUT INTO BITE-SIZE PIECES
1/2	CUP GOLDEN RAISINS
2	RIPE BANANAS
1	CUP LOW-FAT MILK
4	LARGE EGGS, BEATEN
1/4	CUP EGG SUBSTITUTE
1/4	CUP SUGAR
1	TSP CINNAMON

1. Preheat oven to 325°F.

2. Prepare 8 custard dishes with nonstick cooking spray. Evenly distribute the stale bread and the golden raisins into the dishes.

3. Mash bananas. Add milk, beaten egg, egg substitute, sugar, and cinnamon to make custard. Pour custard mixture evenly into each custard dish; place in a large, flat baking pan. Fill pan with hot water, covering 3/4 of the custard dishes, and place in the oven. Bake until custard is set, about 45 minutes. Gently remove from water bath and serve warm.

May
&
June

Spring and a Weekend Adventure

SPRING IS definitely in the air as May and June arrive. The days are longer, and we spend more time outdoors. This is a great time of year to get out and exercise, whether it is simply walking or hiking or maybe even taking a weekend adventure.

My family's favorite activities involve the water. We love both freshwater and saltwater fishing. Fortunately, we're close to both and can enjoy fishing throughout the year! In May and June, however, we go down to the coast with our rods, reels, and casting nets so we can spend some time on the docks of the North and South Carolina coasts. The boys and I have learned how to properly throw a casting net to get bait fish. It's a lot of fun to learn and even more fun when you actually catch something.

Now the boys and I go out to the dock to catch the big fish. Unfortunately, the big fish have yet to be caught. My son tells me that this elusive fish is out there and that it'll take his bait with a mighty tug. I just hope this is the year we catch it! I generally prefer surf casting, where you have a large fishing pole and cast out into the ocean from the shore. You'll usually see surf casters early in the morning, with their poles stuck into the sand. I am one of those, and usually one of my boys is with me. When we were out early one morning last year, we kept getting bites and reeled in black tip sharks. Those sharks were no more than 12 inches long, but beautiful to see up close. We immediately let them back into the water and stood amazed by their beauty.

When you're fishing, there always has to be a meal from your catch! I have used many of the recipes from this chapter on my fishing excursions. A favorite of mine is the Avocado Brochette. I pack the avocado mixture in ice and the bread separately and enjoy every bite with some really cold water. Sometimes, I pack the ingredients for the Chilled Poached Salmon Sandwiches in ice and assemble them right on the dock, so I can taste some fish while I am fishing!

Whether it's a fishing excursion or an afternoon on the golf course, there is plenty to do in May and June. Take the steps to be more active and bring along a friend or family member. Search for your own weekend adventure!

AVOCADO BROCHETTE

1 FRENCH BAGUETTE

2 CUPS AVOCADO, MEDIUM DICE

1/2 CUP PLUM TOMATO, SMALL DICE

2 TBSP MINCED RED ONIONS

1 CLOVE GARLIC, MINCED

1 TBSP OLIVE OIL

1 TSP MINCED FRESH OREGANO

1/2 TSP SALT

PINCH PEPPER

SERVES 16
SERVING SIZE: 1 TBSP

1. Slice French baguette into 1/2-inch-thick slices. Toast and set aside.

2. Combine the remaining ingredients and place onto baguette slices. Serve while hot.

Exchanges/Choices

1 Starch

1 Fat

Basic Nutritional Values

Calories 115

Calories from Fat 40

Total Fat 4.5 g

Saturated Fat 0.7 g

Trans Fat 0 g

Cholesterol 0 mg

Sodium 245 mg

Total Carbohydrate 17 g

Dietary Fiber 2 g

Sugars 0 g

Protein 3 g

CHILLED CANTALOUPE SOUP

SERVES 4
SERVING SIZE: 1/4 RECIPE

3 CUPS RIPE CANTALOUPE, MEDIUM DICE
1/2 CUP APPLE JUICE
1/2 CUP LOW-FAT VANILLA YOGURT
1 TBSP HONEY

Exchanges/Choices
1 1/2 Carbohydrate

Basic Nutritional Values
Calories 100
  Calories from Fat 10
Total Fat 1 g
  Saturated Fat 0.4 g
  Trans Fat 0 g
Cholesterol 0 mg
Sodium 30 mg
Total Carbohydrate 22 g
  Dietary Fiber 1 g
  Sugars 21 g
Protein 2 g

1. Dice the cantaloupe into 1-inch pieces and place them in a food processor. Blend until smooth.

2. Add the apple juice, yogurt, and honey and continue processing until desired consistency is reached. Chill the mixture for 30 minutes.

3. Serve the soup with diced honeydew or other melon.

CREAM OF VIDALIA ONION SOUP

1	TBSP OLIVE OIL
3	CUPS VIDALIA ONIONS, SLICED
2	CLOVES GARLIC, MINCED
1 1/2	QUARTS CHICKEN STOCK (SEE RECIPE ON P. 24)
2	CUPS PEELED, DICED POTATOES
4	SPRIGS FRESH THYME
1	CUP FAT-FREE HALF & HALF
2	TSP SALT
1/2	TSP WHITE PEPPER
1/4	CUP SCALLIONS, SLICED

SERVES 8
SERVING SIZE: 1/8 RECIPE

Exchanges/Choices
1 Carbohydrate
1/2 Fat

Basic Nutritional Values
Calories 100
  Calories from Fat 20
Total Fat 2.5 g
  Saturated Fat 0.6 g
  Trans Fat 0 g
Cholesterol 5 mg
Sodium 625 mg
Total Carbohydrate 17 g
  Dietary Fiber 2 g
  Sugars 5 g
Protein 3 g

In a large pot, heat olive oil. Add Vidalia onions and slowly cook until onions are soft and translucent but not browned. Add minced garlic, chicken stock, diced potatoes, and thyme. Bring to a low simmer and cook until potatoes are tender, about 25 minutes. Remove thyme and blend liquid until smooth. Return to pot and add half & half; season with salt and pepper. Bring back to a simmer and stir. Remove from heat, garnish with fresh scallions, and serve.

Spinach Salad with Tangerines, Onions, and Walnuts

Serves 6
Serving size: 1/6 recipe

1	LB FRESH SPINACH, CLEANED AND WASHED
1/4	CUP TANGERINE VINAIGRETTE (SEE RECIPE ON P. 31)
2	TANGERINES, CUT INTO SEGMENTS
1	SMALL RED ONION, PEELED AND SLICED
1/4	CUP WALNUTS, COARSELY CHOPPED
2	HARD-BOILED EGGS, CHOPPED
2	BACON STRIPS, COOKED AND DICED SMALL

Make sure all ingredients are prepped and chilled. Place spinach in a large bowl, add tangerine vinaigrette, and toss to coat spinach. Divide spinach evenly into six serving dishes. Garnish with tangerine segments, red onion, walnuts, eggs, and bacon. Serve immediately.

Exchanges/Choices
1/2 Fruit
1 Vegetable
2 Fat

Basic Nutritional Values
Calories 150
  Calories from Fat 90
Total Fat 10 g
  Saturated Fat 1.5 g
  Trans Fat 0 g
Cholesterol 75 mg
Sodium 210 mg
Total Carbohydrate 11 g
  Dietary Fiber 3 g
  Sugars 6 g
Protein 6 g

CHILLED POACHED SALMON SANDWICHES

Poaching liquid

2	CUPS WHITE WINE
2	CUPS WATER
1	MEDIUM ONION, CUT INTO QUARTERS
4	SPRIGS FRESH THYME
1/2	TSP WHOLE PEPPERCORNS
2	BAY LEAVES
1	LEMON WEDGE, SEEDS REMOVED

Sandwich

4	SALMON FILLETS (4 OZ EACH)
2	TBSP CAPERS
3 3/4	TBSP LIGHT MAYONNAISE
4	KAISER ROLLS
1/4	CUP RED ONION, SLICED

SERVES 4
SERVING SIZE: 1 SANDWICH

Exchanges/Choices

2 Starch
4 Lean Meat
1 Fat

Basic Nutritional Values

Calories 380
  Calories from Fat 115
Total Fat 13 g
  Saturated Fat 2.4 g
  Trans Fat 0 g
Cholesterol 55 mg
Sodium 590 mg
Total Carbohydrate 32 g
  Dietary Fiber 2 g
  Sugars 3 g
Protein 30 g

1. Combine all poaching liquid ingredients and bring to a simmer in a large shallow pan. Place salmon fillets evenly into poaching liquid, making sure that the salmon is submerged. Bring liquid back to a simmer and cook for another 10 minutes or until done. Remove fillets from poaching liquid and set aside to cool.

2. When salmon fillets have cooled, assemble sandwiches. Combine the capers and mayonnaise; spread on kaiser rolls. Place salmon fillets on rolls. Arrange sliced onions on top and serve.

Scallops in White Wine Sauce

SERVES 4
SERVING SIZE: 1/4 RECIPE

Exchanges/Choices
1 Carbohydrate
1 Lean Meat
1 Fat

Basic Nutritional Values
Calories 150
  Calories from Fat 45
Total Fat 9 g
  Saturated Fat 1.3 g
  Trans Fat 0 g
Cholesterol 115 mg
Sodium 325 mg
Total Carbohydrate 11 g
  Dietary Fiber 2 g
  Sugars 6 g
Protein 27 g

1/4	CUP FRESH BREAD CRUMBS
2	TBSP FRESHLY GRATED PARMESAN CHEESE
1	TBSP OLIVE OIL
8	SEA SCALLOPS, MUSCLE REMOVED
2	TBSP SHALLOTS, SMALL DICE
1	CUP DRY WHITE WINE
1	CUP FAT-FREE HALF & HALF
1	TSP MINCED FRESH THYME
	BLACK PEPPER, TO TASTE
2	TBSP PILLSBURY SHAKER FLOUR
1	TBSP MINCED FRESH PARSLEY

1. Place fresh bread crumbs on a sheet pan; put in a 350°F oven. Toast crumbs to a golden brown, about 6–8 minutes. Remove and set aside to cool. When bread crumbs are completely cooled, add Parmesan cheese and combine thoroughly. Set aside.

2. Heat a medium skillet and add olive oil. Place scallops in pan and sear until golden brown. Turn over and sear other side until golden brown; then remove and set aside.

3. Add shallots to pan and sweat. Deglaze with white wine and reduce by half. Add half & half and bring to a low simmer. Add fresh thyme and black pepper to taste. Add shaker flour to bring sauce to a light thickness. Add scallops to pan and finish cooking, about 2 minutes. Scallops should be slightly firm to the touch.

4. Place two scallops on each scallop shell and place in a baking dish or oven-safe dish. Pour 2 Tbsp of sauce over scallops, then sprinkle bread crumb mixture over scallops, and broil until golden brown, about 1 minute. Garnish with parsley and serve.

LASAGNA ROLLS

9   OZ LOW-FAT RICOTTA CHEESE

2   LARGE EGGS, BEATEN

2   TSP FRESH OREGANO, FINELY CHOPPED

1/2   TSP BLACK PEPPER

2   TBSP FRESHLY GRATED PARMESAN CHEESE

1   TBSP MINCED FRESH PARSLEY

6   LASAGNA NOODLES, COOKED

2   CUPS MARINARA SAUCE (SEE RECIPE ON P. 18)

SERVES 6
SERVING SIZE: 1/6 RECIPE

1. Preheat oven to 375°F. In a medium bowl, combine the ricotta cheese, eggs, oregano, pepper, Parmesan cheese, and parsley. Set aside.

2. On a clean, flat surface, lay out the lasagna noodles. Evenly spread cheese mixture on top of each lasagna noodle, leaving about 1 inch uncovered on one end of each noodle. Beginning with the cheese end, gently roll up the noodles.

3. Place the marinara sauce in an ovenproof baking dish. Place the lasagna rolls seam-side down in the dish and cover. Bake for about 45 minutes, until sauce is lightly bubbling.

Exchanges/Choices
1 1/2 Starch
1 Lean Meat
1/2 Fat

Basic Nutritional Values
Calories 185
  Calories from Fat 55
Total Fat 6 g
  Saturated Fat 2.4 g
  Trans Fat 0 g
Cholesterol 85 mg
Sodium 275 mg
Total Carbohydrate 23 g
  Dietary Fiber 2 g
  Sugars 5 g
Protein 11 g

Tips for the Kitchen

To cook lasagna, bring 2 quarts of water to a boil in a large pot. Add the lasagna noodles and stir gently. Cook according to package directions. Drain the cooked pasta and cool by running under cold water. Set aside.

GLAZED BLOOD ORANGE PORK CHOPS

SERVES 4
SERVING SIZE: 1 PORK CHOP

Exchanges/Choices
1/2 Fruit
4 Lean Meat
1 1/2 Fat

Basic Nutritional Values
Calories 265
Calories from Fat 125
Total Fat 14 g
Saturated Fat 3.5 g
Trans Fat 0 g
Cholesterol 70 mg
Sodium 55 mg
Total Carbohydrate 9 g
Dietary Fiber 0 g
Sugars 7 g
Protein 25 g

2	TBSP OLIVE OIL
1/2	TSP MARJORAM, CRUSHED
1/2	TSP COARSE GROUND BLACK PEPPER
2	TSP BLOOD ORANGE ZEST
4	PORK CHOPS (6 OZ EACH), TRIMMED OF FAT
1	TBSP MINCED SHALLOTS
1	CUP BLOOD ORANGE JUICE
1	TSP BROWN SUGAR
5	SPRIGS FRESH THYME

1. Combine olive oil, marjoram, black pepper, and blood orange zest. Marinate pork chops and refrigerate for at least 2 hours.

2. Preheat a large skillet and sear pork chops until golden brown on both sides. Remove pork and set aside.

3. Add shallots to pan and sweat them, stirring often. Deglaze with blood orange juice. Add brown sugar and fresh thyme; bring to a simmer. Place pork chops back into pan and reduce heat to low. Continue to cook pork chops on low heat for about 45 minutes or until pork chops are very tender.

4. Once pork chops are cooked (160°F internal temperature) and tender, remove them from the pan and increase heat. Continue heating liquid until it has reduced to a syrupy consistency. Place pork chops back into pan to coat with orange glaze. Serve immediately.

Tips for the Kitchen
If you can't find blood oranges, just use regular oranges in the same amounts.

SHRIMP AND GRITS

1 LB SHRIMP, CLEANED AND SHELLS REMOVED

1 TSP PAPRIKA

1 TSP MINCED FRESH THYME

2 TSP LEMON ZEST

  PINCH BLACK PEPPER

1 CUP SHRIMP STOCK (SEE RECIPE ON P. 26 OR
    SUBSTITUTE CHICKEN STOCK ON P. 24)

2 CUPS LOW-FAT MILK

1 CUP WHITE CORNMEAL

1 TBSP OLIVE OIL

1/2 CUP SLICED ONIONS

1/2 CUP SLICED RED PEPPERS

1/4 CUP SLICED SCALLIONS

SERVES 4
SERVING SIZE: 1/4 RECIPE

Exchanges/Choices
2 Starch
1/2 Fat-Free Milk
2 Lean Meat
1 Fat

Basic Nutritional Values
Calories 325
Calories from Fat 80
Total Fat 9 g
Saturated Fat 2 g
Trans Fat 0 g
Cholesterol 140 mg
Sodium 220 mg
Total Carbohydrate 37 g
Dietary Fiber 3 g
Sugars 8 g
Protein 22 g

1. Combine the raw shrimp, paprika, fresh thyme, lemon zest, and black pepper; marinate for 2 hours.

2. In a medium pot, bring the shrimp stock and milk to a simmer. In a steady stream, pour in cornmeal, stirring as you pour. Reduce heat to a low simmer. Cook until mixture has thickened and cornmeal is smooth and creamy. Add additional stock if needed.

3. Meanwhile bring a sauté pan to medium-high heat. Add olive oil and marinated shrimp. Sauté until fully cooked, about 5–8 minutes. Remove shrimp from pan and set aside. In the same pan, add onions and peppers and sauté until the onions are a light golden color. Return shrimp to pan and toss together. Pour shrimp mixture into grits; stir to incorporate. Garnish with scallions and serve immediately.

CHICKEN QUESADILLAS

SERVES 4
SERVING SIZE: 1 QUESADILLA

8	OZ SKINLESS, BONELESS CHICKEN BREASTS
1	TSP GROUND SAGE
1	TSP GROUND ROSEMARY
1	TBSP MINCED GARLIC
1	TBSP OLIVE OIL
	COOKING SPRAY
4	TORTILLAS (10 INCHES EACH)
1/2	CUP FAT-FREE CHEDDAR CHEESE, GRATED
1/2	CUP FAT-FREE MOZZARELLA CHEESE, GRATED
1	MEDIUM TOMATO, DICED
1/2	CUP DICED RED PEPPERS
2	TSP MINCED JALAPEÑO

Exchanges/Choices
2 1/2 Starch
3 Lean Meat
1 Fat

Basic Nutritional Values
Calories 370
  Calories from Fat 90
Total Fat 10 g
  Saturated Fat 2.2 g
  Trans Fat 0 g
Cholesterol 35 mg
Sodium 785 mg
Total Carbohydrate 41 g
  Dietary Fiber 3 g
  Sugars 4 g
Protein 27 g

This recipe is
high in sodium.

1. Slice the raw chicken into very thin strips and place in a medium bowl. Add sage, rosemary, garlic, and olive oil. Combine thoroughly. Let marinate in refrigerator overnight.

2. Heat a large nonstick skillet over medium-high heat. Spray the skillet with cooking spray. Add the chicken strips and stir-fry quickly until evenly browned and fully cooked. Set aside.

3. Preheat oven to 375°F. Place two tortillas on a clean, flat sheet pan. Spread the two cheeses evenly over the tortillas. Sprinkle diced tomatoes, red pepper, and jalapeño on top of the cheeses. Divide the chicken strips evenly on the tortillas. Use remaining tortillas to cover each quesadilla. Bake in the oven for 10 minutes or until cheese is melted.

4. Slice each quesadilla into four sections and serve hot.

Tips for the Kitchen
You can make this dish on the stove top, as well. Place the filled quesadillas in a preheated pan coated with cooking spray and cook until golden on bottom. Carefully turn over and brown the other side.

POACHED SALMON WITH LEEKS

4	CUPS FISH STOCK (SEE RECIPE ON P. 25)
1/2	CUP DICED ONIONS
1/2	CUP DICED CELERY
4	SALMON FILLETS (4 OZ EACH)
1	TBSP OLIVE OIL
2	CUPS LEEKS, WASHED, DRIED, AND THINLY SLICED
2	TSP MINCED FRESH THYME
1	TBSP FRESH LEMON JUICE
	DASH PEPPER

SERVES 4
SERVING SIZE: 1 FILLET

1. In a large shallow pan, add fish stock, onions, and celery and bring to a simmer. Add salmon fillets; bring to a low simmer. Be sure the fillets are fully submerged, so they can properly poach. Cook until done, about 10–15 minutes, depending on thickness.

2. While salmon cooks, add olive oil to a sauté pan over medium heat. Add leeks and sauté until they are soft and tender, being sure not to brown them, about 8–10 minutes. Add 1/4 cup of fish stock (from the poached salmon), thyme, and lemon juice.

3. When leeks are done, remove from the pan, arrange on a serving dish, and season with pepper. Place poached salmon on top; serve.

Exchanges/Choices
1 Vegetable
3 Lean Meat
1 Fat

Basic Nutritional Values
Calories 225
  Calories from Fat 90
Total Fat 10 g
  Saturated Fat 1.9 g
  Trans Fat 0 g
Cholesterol 50 mg
Sodium 60 mg
Total Carbohydrate 7 g
  Dietary Fiber 1 g
  Sugars 2 g
Protein 25 g

Tips for the Kitchen

Here's how to clean leeks. Remove the dark green leaves and roots; discard. Slice in half lengthwise and place in 2 quarts of cold water. Soak for a few minutes to remove dirt and sand. Repeat as needed.

BASIC PIEROGI DOUGH

SERVES 20
SERVING SIZE: 1 PIEROGI

2	CUPS WHOLE-WHEAT FLOUR, SIFTED
	PINCH SALT
1	LARGE EGG
1/2	CUP COLD WATER

Exchanges/Choices
1/2 Starch

Basic Nutritional Values
Calories 45
  Calories from Fat 0
Total Fat 0 g
  Saturated Fat 0.1 g
  Trans Fat 0 g
Cholesterol 10 mg
Sodium 0 mg
Total Carbohydrate 9 g
  Dietary Fiber 1 g
  Sugars 0 g
Protein 2 g

1. On a clean cooking service, sift whole-wheat flour and make a well. Add salt and egg. Using a fork, gently whisk egg, slowly incorporating flour from the edges. In a slow steady stream, pour cold water into well and continue to combine ingredients until a dough forms. Knead dough until smooth and round. Place a damp cloth or bowl over dough and let it rest for 10 minutes.

2. Cut away half of the dough and roll out until thin and even. Use a cutter or drinking glass and cut out round disks of dough.

3. Stuff dough with your chosen filling. You can use sautéed onions (see recipe on p. 113), potato and cheddar (see recipe on p. 114), or sauerkraut (see recipe on p. 115). Fold the dough over the filling and, using a fork, press dough together to seal. If you have one, you can also use a pierogi press to make this step go faster.

4. Bring a large pot of water to a boil, add a pinch of salt, and place small batches of pierogis into water, being careful not to crowd them. Lower heat to a simmer and cook for 8–10 minutes, until tender and fully cooked. Remove from water and serve hot.

SAUTÉED ONION PIEROGI FILLING

1 TBSP OLIVE OIL

2 CUPS SLICED ONIONS

1. In a large skillet, heat the olive oil. Add sliced onions. Over medium heat, cook onions until golden brown in color.

2. Fold onions into pierogi dough, then sauté stuffed pierogis until golden brown. Serve hot.

Exchanges/Choices
Free Food

Basic Nutritional Values
Calories 15
  Calories from Fat 5
Total Fat 0.5 g
  Saturated Fat 0.1 g
  Trans Fat 0 g
Cholesterol 0 mg
Sodium 0 mg
Total Carbohydrate 2 g
  Dietary Fiber 0 g
  Sugars 1 g
Protein 0 g

This nutritional data is for the filling only.

POTATO AND CHEDDAR PIEROGI FILLING

SERVES 20
SERVING SIZE: 1 PIEROGI

1/2	CUP ONIONS, SMALL DICE
1	TBSP OLIVE OIL
1	LB RED BLISS POTATOES, PEELED AND QUARTERED
1/2	TSP SALT
	PINCH WHITE PEPPER
1	CUP SHARP CHEDDAR CHEESE, GRATED

1. Sauté onions in olive oil until tender and soft; avoid browning. Set aside to cool.

2. In a medium saucepan, cover the potatoes with water and boil until fully cooked, about 15 minutes. Drain well and mash until smooth. Fold in onions, salt, pepper, and cheese.

Exchanges/Choices
1/2 Starch
1/2 Fat

Basic Nutritional Values
Calories 45
  Calories from Fat 20
Total Fat 2.5 g
  Saturated Fat 1.3 g
  Trans Fat 0 g
Cholesterol 0 mg
Sodium 95 mg
Total Carbohydrate 4 g
  Dietary Fiber 0 g
  Sugars 1 g
Protein 2 g

This nutritional data is for the filling only.

Sauerkraut Pierogi Filling

14	OZ SAUERKRAUT
1	TBSP BUTTER
1/4	CUP ONION, SMALL DICE
1/2	TSP SALT
	PINCH BLACK PEPPER

SERVES 20
SERVING SIZE: 1 PIEROGI

1. Thoroughly drain sauerkraut and chop finely; set aside.

2. In a skillet, heat butter. Add onions and sweat. Add sauerkraut and continue to cook on low heat for 10 minutes, until fully cooked and tender. Season with salt and pepper. Set aside until needed.

Exchanges/Choices
Free Food

Basic Nutritional Values
Calories 10
  Calories from Fat 5
Total Fat 0.5 g
  Saturated Fat 0.4 g
  Trans Fat 0 g
Cholesterol 0 mg
Sodium 140 mg
Total Carbohydrate 1 g
  Dietary Fiber 1 g
  Sugars 0 g
Protein 0 g

This nutritional data is for the filling only.

SHRIMP AND SWEET PEA RISOTTO

SERVES 6
SERVING SIZE: 1/6 RECIPE

Exchanges/Choices
2 Starch
2 Lean Meat
1 Fat

Basic Nutritional Values

Calories 285
  Calories from Fat 100
Total Fat 11 g
  Saturated Fat 3 g
  Trans Fat 0 g
Cholesterol 120 mg
Sodium 210 mg
Total Carbohydrate 29 g
  Dietary Fiber 2 g
  Sugars 3 g
Protein 17 g

2	TBSP OLIVE OIL
1	MEDIUM ONION, SMALL DICE
2	TBSP MINCED GARLIC
1	CUP ARBORIO RICE
1/4	CUP WHITE WINE
3	CUPS HOT CHICKEN STOCK (SEE RECIPE ON P. 24)
1	CUP SWEET PEA PUREE (SEE RECIPE ON P. 117)
	BLACK PEPPER, TO TASTE
1	LB PEELED LARGE SHRIMP
1	TBSP MINCED FRESH TARRAGON
1/4	CUP SHAVED ROMANO CHEESE

1. Preheat a heavy-bottomed pot; add 1 Tbsp olive oil. Add diced onion and 1 Tbsp garlic; sweat until soft. Add rice and stir to incorporate, until rice is coated (this will help the rice absorb the liquids).

2. Add white wine and simmer for 2–3 minutes or until wine is about three-quarters absorbed. Lower heat to lowest setting and add 1 cup of chicken stock to cover rice. Smooth over the surface of the rice with a spoon to ensure even cooking. When the liquid is absorbed by the rice, add another cup of stock to the risotto and continue stirring. Repeat process with the last cup of stock. Make sure that the rice does not stick to the bottom of the pan. Continue this process for 20 minutes or until rice is almost fully cooked.

3. When the rice has absorbed the stock and is tender and fully cooked, add the sweet pea puree and black pepper; stir to incorporate.

4. Preheat a sauté pan and add 1 Tbsp olive oil. Add remaining garlic and shrimp and quickly sauté. Toss in tarragon and finish cooking. Cook until shrimp are firm to the touch, about 5–8 minutes. Set aside.

5. Portion risotto evenly into six serving bowls. Add sautéed shrimp on top and garnish with shaved Romano cheese. Serve immediately.

Sweet Pea Puree

1   Tbsp olive oil

2   tsp minced garlic

6   oz peas, frozen

3   oz chicken stock (see recipe on p. 24)

1   tsp butter

Serves 8
Serving size: 2 Tbsp

1. In a small pan, heat the olive oil. Add garlic and sauté for 2–3 minutes. Add peas and chicken stock; simmer until peas are just tender, about 3–5 minutes. Remove peas from heat, transfer to a blender, and puree. (Be careful of hot liquid.)

2. Add butter and stir into peas. Keep warm on the stove until needed or store in the freezer for up to 2 months.

Exchanges/Choices

1 Vegetable
1/2 Fat

Basic Nutritional Values

Calories 45
 Calories from Fat 25
Total Fat 3 g
 Saturated Fat 1.2 g
 Trans Fat 0 g
Cholesterol 5 mg
Sodium 30 mg
Total Carbohydrate 3 g
 Dietary Fiber 1 g
 Sugars 1 g
Protein 1 g

CHILLED LEMON ASPARAGUS

SERVES 6
SERVING SIZE: 1/6 RECIPE

3   CUPS WATER
1/2   TSP SALT
1   LB ASPARAGUS
   JUICE OF 1 LEMON
1   TBSP EXTRA-VIRGIN OLIVE OIL
   PEPPER, TO TASTE

Exchanges/Choices
1 Vegetable
1/2 Fat

Basic Nutritional Values
Calories 40
  Calories from Fat 20
Total Fat 2.5 g
  Saturated Fat 0.3 g
  Trans Fat 0 g
Cholesterol 0 mg
Sodium 50 mg
Total Carbohydrate 3 g
  Dietary Fiber 1 g
  Sugars 1 g
Protein 2 g

1. Bring water to a boil in a large skillet. Add salt and asparagus. Cover and cook asparagus for 2 minutes or until slightly tender.

2. Drain water and chill rapidly in an ice bath. (To make an ice bath, fill a large container with 2 cups of ice and add 4 cups of water.) Once asparagus is cooled, drain thoroughly and pat dry.

3. Place asparagus on a serving dish. Pour lemon juice over asparagus. Drizzle with olive oil and season with pepper. Serve chilled.

CHOCOLATE BERRY PURSES

3   SHEETS PHYLLO DOUGH
    COOKING SPRAY
1   PINT FRESH RASPBERRIES
4   TSP CHOCOLATE CHIPS

SERVES 6
SERVING SIZE: 1 PIECE

1. Preheat oven to 375°F.

2. On a clean work surface, lay out one sheet of phyllo dough and spray for 1 second with cooking spray. Place a second sheet directly on top of first sheet of phyllo; repeat spray. Place third sheet directly on top of second sheet of phyllo and spray again.

3. Using a sharp knife, make a center slice horizontally. Then cut phyllo into thirds vertically, so you end up with six even squares.

4. Place three raspberries on top of each phyllo square. Evenly divide chocolate chips over raspberries.

5. Bring corners of the phyllo squares together, thus wrapping up the ingredients. Gently twist the corners together to seal shut.

6. Arrange chocolate berry purses evenly on a baking pan and bake until phyllo is golden brown, about 10 minutes. Serve warm.

Exchanges/Choices
1 Carbohydrate

Basic Nutritional Values
Calories 70
  Calories from Fat 15
Total Fat 1.5 g
  Saturated Fat 0.4 g
  Trans Fat 0 g
Cholesterol 0 mg
Sodium 45 mg
Total Carbohydrate 14 g
  Dietary Fiber 3 g
  Sugars 3 g
Protein 1 g

BLUEBERRY CRISP

SERVES 6
SERVING SIZE: 1/6 RECIPE

Exchanges/Choices
2 1/2 Carbohydrate
1 Fat

Basic Nutritional Values
Calories 205
  Calories from Fat 55
Total Fat 6 g
  Saturated Fat 0.9 g
  Trans Fat 0 g
Cholesterol 0 mg
Sodium 70 mg
Total Carbohydrate 38 g
  Dietary Fiber 5 g
  Sugars 19 g
Protein 3 g

Blueberry mix

1/2	CUP WATER
2	TBSP SPLENDA SUGAR BLEND FOR BAKING
3	CUPS BLUEBERRIES
2	TSP MINCED FRESH MINT

Topping

1	CUP WHOLE-WHEAT FLOUR, SIFTED
2	TBSP SPLENDA SUGAR BLEND FOR BAKING
2	TBSP SPLENDA BROWN SUGAR BLEND
2	TSP CINNAMON
4	TBSP WHIPPED MARGARINE
	COOKING SPRAY

1. Prepare the blueberry mix. Over medium heat, bring water to a simmer. Add Splenda; stir until dissolved, and then add blueberries. Lower the heat and cook until blueberries begin to pop but retain their shape. Remove from heat immediately and add mint.

2. Incorporate all the dry topping ingredients (except margarine). Then, using your hands, mix the margarine with the dry ingredients until well incorporated and a crumbly texture is created.

3. Using nonstick cooking spray, coat 6 small oven-safe ramekins. Pour equal amounts of the blueberry mixture into each and then cover with the crumb topping. Bake at 325°F, until slightly brown and bubbling around the sides, about 25 minutes.

STRAWBERRIES AND FIGS WITH PORT

1 PINT FRESH STRAWBERRIES, WASHED AND
   STEMS REMOVED

12 FRESH FIGS

1 1/2 CUPS PORT WINE

FAT-FREE WHIPPED TOPPING (OPTIONAL)

FRESH MINT (OPTIONAL)

SERVES 6
SERVING SIZE: 1/6 RECIPE

1. Wash the fruit and pat dry. Remove the stems from the strawberries and slice them into quarters. Divide the quartered strawberries evenly among six large-rimmed wine glasses. Cut the figs into quarters. Divide them evenly among the wine glasses and layer over the berries.

2. Pour 1/4 cup of the port wine into each glass. If desired, top with a dollop of whipped topping and a sprig of fresh mint.

Exchanges/Choices
2 Carbohydrate

Basic Nutritional Values
Calories 155
  Calories from Fat 0
Total Fat 0 g
  Saturated Fat 0.1 g
  Trans Fat 0 g
Cholesterol 0 mg
Sodium 5 mg
Total Carbohydrate 29 g
  Dietary Fiber 4 g
  Sugars 14 g
Protein 1 g

STRAWBERRY PEAR CHUTNEY

SERVES 4
SERVING SIZE: 1/4 CUP

1	PINT FRESH STRAWBERRIES, WASHED, HULLED, AND DICED
1	SMALL BOSC PEAR, DICED
1	TBSP FRESH MINT, CHIFFONADE
1/4	CUP CHOPPED WALNUTS
1	TBSP HONEY
	ZEST OF 1 LEMON

In a medium bowl, combine the strawberries, pear, mint, walnuts, honey, and lemon zest. Chill in the refrigerator until needed.

Exchanges/Choices
1 Fruit
1 Fat

Basic Nutritional Values
Calories 110
  Calories from Fat 45
Total Fat 5 g
  Saturated Fat 0.5 g
  Trans Fat 0 g
Cholesterol 0 mg
Sodium 0 mg
Total Carbohydrate 17 g
  Dietary Fiber 4 g
  Sugars 12 g
Protein 2 g

July
&
August

FLAVORS OF THE FOURTH

THE FOURTH of July has always been a special holiday for me. I grew up in the '70s in suburban New York, so July and August were always hot and unpleasant! Backyard pools were open, and staying up past your normal bedtime was okay. Baseball was in mid-season, and we were out of school for the summer. Yes, the Fourth was the celebration for kids to welcome summer.

Independence Day has always been fun because we would traditionally have a party at my house. We would have over at least 20 people. There would be the classic picnic table filled with potato and macaroni salad, a big green salad, chips and dips, pickles, tomatoes, and, of course, the big watermelon cut in half with assorted fruits. My dad, or "Padre," as I called him, had a big shaded tarp to protect those who did not want to sit in the hot rays of the sun. We also had some shade over the pool, so there was always a cool spot to swim in.

Then, when all of our friends and neighbors had arrived, Padre would start the grill. This was in the days of charcoal and lighter fluid. The black plume of smoke and the gassy scent of newly lit fire filled the corner where Padre and the other men would cluster, enjoying their beer and laughing heartily. It was always a good time. This was a party, this was summer, this was a celebration, this was the Fourth of July!

As the coals turned to white ash and the spit of fire subsided, the meats would be put on the grill racks. Burgers and dogs would go on first. Padre walked around to everybody, asking "burger or dog," and people had to respond with a number. One was burger. Two was hot dog. Later on, Padre would put on his special marinated pork ribs, which sweetly scented the air as they grilled. They were succulent when you ate them, as mouthwatering as they smelled. To this day we still make them, and they are included in my first cookbook.

We ate and talked and laughed. Every year, we toasted to freedom and the United States. Every one of us in our own way recognized the sacrifices that had been made in order for us to celebrate the holiday. When you celebrate our country's independence, take a moment this Fourth and think of those who are still fighting for our freedom. Think of the men and women who answered the call to defend our way of life, of their interrupted lives, of their careers on hold, and of their praying families waiting for a safe return. To all of you who have made these sacrifices and to all who have made the ultimate sacrifice: thank you.

Mexican-Style Shrimp Cocktail

8 oz Clamato juice

Juice of 1 lemon

1/4 cup ketchup

1 cup shrimp stock (see recipe on p. 26)

1 lb cooked shrimp, medium dice

1 cup cucumbers, peeled and seeded, small dice

1 small red onion, small dice

1 medium tomato, diced and seeded

1 avocado, small dice

1 tsp minced jalapeño

1 Tbsp minced cilantro

1 Tbsp minced parsley

Serves 6
Serving size: 1/6 recipe

1. Combine Clamato, lemon juice, ketchup, and shrimp stock and refrigerate.

2. Place 2 Tbsp of shrimp into a serving glass. Layer with cucumber, red onion, tomato, avocado, and jalapeño. Repeat layering with shrimp and vegetables. Evenly pour ketchup mixture over each serving and chill for 30 minutes. Garnish with minced cilantro and parsley and serve.

Exchanges/Choices
2 Vegetable
2 Lean Meat
1/2 Fat

Basic Nutritional Values
Calories 155
 Calories from Fat 40
Total Fat 4.5 g
 Saturated Fat 0.8 g
 Trans Fat 0 g
Cholesterol 150 mg
Sodium 445 mg
Total Carbohydrate 10 g
 Dietary Fiber 3 g
 Sugars 4 g
Protein 17 g

Sweet Pea with Tarragon Soup

Serves 6
Serving size: 1/6 recipe

Exchanges/Choices
1 Starch
1/2 Fat

Basic Nutritional Values
Calories 90
  Calories from Fat 25
Total Fat 3 g
  Saturated Fat 0.7 g
  Trans Fat 0 g
Cholesterol 5 mg
Sodium 265 mg
Total Carbohydrate 12 g
  Dietary Fiber 4 g
  Sugars 5 g
Protein 4 g

1	Tbsp olive oil
1/2	cup diced onions
1/2	tsp salt
	Pinch ground pepper
1	lb frozen peas
4	cups chicken stock (see recipe on p. 24)
4	Tbsp crème fraîche
2	Tbsp fresh tarragon

1. Preheat a medium pot over medium heat. Add olive oil and onions; sauté until just translucent. Season with salt and pepper. Add peas and chicken stock; bring to a simmer.

2. Simmer for about 10 minutes or until peas are soft but retain a bright green color. Remove from heat and blend liquid in a food processor or blender. If soup becomes too thick, thin out with more chicken stock.

3. Once pea soup is pureed, strain through a sieve or fine-mesh strainer. Set aside.

4. Pour pea soup into small serving bowls. Add a dollop of crème fraîche (you can purchase this in your local store or make it at home), garnish with tarragon, and serve.

SIMPLE SALSA

6 RIPE PLUM TOMATOES, PEELED, SEEDED,
    SMALL DICE
1/2 CUP RED ONIONS, SMALL DICE
1 TSP MINCED JALAPEÑO PEPPERS
2 CLOVES GARLIC, MINCED
2 TBSP CHOPPED FRESH CILANTRO
2 TSP GRATED LIME ZEST
2 TBSP LIME JUICE, FRESH SQUEEZED
2 TSP CUMIN
FRESH GROUND PEPPER, TO TASTE
PINCH SALT

SERVES 3
SERVING SIZE: 1/3 RECIPE

In a large bowl, gently combine the tomatoes, onions, jalapeños, garlic, cilantro, lime zest, and lime juice. Season with cumin, pepper, and salt. Cover and refrigerate for 1 hour. Serve chilled.

Exchanges/Choices
2 Vegetable

Basic Nutritional Values
Calories 55
  Calories from Fat 5
Total Fat 0.5 g
  Saturated Fat 0.1 g
  Trans Fat 0 g
Cholesterol 0 mg
Sodium 15 mg
Total Carbohydrate 12 g
  Dietary Fiber 3 g
  Sugars 6 g
Protein 2 g

NECTARINE AND JICAMA SALSA

SERVES 36
SERVING SIZE: 1/4 CUP

6	NECTARINES, CUT INTO SEGMENTS
1	CUP JICAMA ROOT, PEELED AND DICED SMALL
1/4	CUP GRATED COCONUT
1/2	CUP GOLDEN RAISINS
1	TBSP JALAPEÑO PEPPER, SEEDED AND MINCED
1	MEDIUM RED ONION, FINELY DICED
1	TBSP MINCED FRESH CILANTRO
1/4	CUP ORANGE JUICE

Exchanges/Choices
Free Food

Basic Nutritional Values
Calories 20
  Calories from Fat 0
Total Fat 0 g
  Saturated Fat 0.1 g
  Trans Fat 0 g
Cholesterol 0 mg
Sodium 0 mg
Total Carbohydrate 5 g
  Dietary Fiber 1 g
  Sugars 4 g
Protein 0 g

1. Peel the nectarines and slice into sections. Dice jicama into small pieces, about 1/4 inch each.

2. Place all ingredients into a bowl and mix gently. Refrigerate and serve chilled.

Tips for the Kitchen

Jicama is found in most grocery stores in the fresh vegetables section. It has a thin brown skin and is crisp and juicy. It can be served raw or cooked like a potato. Jicama is sometimes called a Mexican potato or Mexican turnip.

Cantaloupe Salsa

2   CUPS CANTALOUPE, SMALL DICE

1/4   CUP RED ONIONS, SMALL DICE

1/2   CUP CHOPPED PECANS

1   TBSP MINCED JALAPEÑO PEPPERS

1/4   CUP HONEY

2   TBSP MINT, CHIFFONADE

Combine all ingredients. Chill for 1 hour and serve.

SERVES 12
SERVING SIZE: 1/4 CUP

Exchanges/Choices
1/2 Carbohydrate
1/2 Fat

Basic Nutritional Values
Calories 65
  Calories from Fat 30
Total Fat 3.5 g
  Saturated Fat 0.3 g
  Trans Fat 0 g
Cholesterol 0 mg
Sodium 0 mg
Total Carbohydrate 9 g
  Dietary Fiber 1 g
  Sugars 8 g
Protein 1 g

ROASTED CORN AND RED PEPPER SALSA

SERVES 6
SERVING SIZE: 1/6 RECIPE

Exchanges/Choices
1 1/2 Starch
1 Vegetable
1/2 Fat

Basic Nutritional Values
Calories 150
  Calories from Fat 55
Total Fat 6 g
  Saturated Fat 0.8 g
  Trans Fat 0 g
Cholesterol 0 mg
Sodium 10 mg
Total Carbohydrate 27 g
  Dietary Fiber 4 g
  Sugars 6 g
Protein 4 g

6	EARS CORN, HUSKED
2	ROASTED RED PEPPERS, CHOPPED (SEE RECIPE ON P. 29)
1	MEDIUM RED ONION, SMALL DICE
2	TSP JALAPEÑO PEPPERS, SEEDED AND DICED
2	CLOVES GARLIC, MINCED
2	TBSP FRESH LEMON JUICE
2	TBSP EXTRA-VIRGIN OLIVE OIL
1	TBSP CHOPPED CILANTRO
2	TSP CUMIN
	BLACK PEPPER, TO TASTE
	PINCH SALT

1. Preheat an outdoor grill. Place corn onto grill and cook until bright yellow and marked with grill marks, about 10–12 minutes. Remove from grill and allow cobs to cool. Cut the kernels from the cobs and reserve in a medium bowl.

2. Place all of the ingredients in a bowl and combine. Cover and refrigerate for 1 hour. Serve chilled.

PINEAPPLE MANGO SALSA

2 CUPS FRESH PINEAPPLE, SMALL DICE

1 CUP DICED MANGO

1/2 CUP RED ONIONS, SMALL DICE

1 CUP PECANS, COARSELY CHOPPED

1/2 CUP DRIED CRANBERRIES

1/4 CUP LIME JUICE, FRESH SQUEEZED

1 TBSP FRESH CILANTRO, CHOPPED

2 TBSP FRESH MINT, CHOPPED

2 TSP JALAPEÑO PEPPERS, SEEDED, SMALL DICE

PINCH SALT

SERVES 6
SERVING SIZE: 1/6 RECIPE

Combine all ingredients in a large bowl. Stir to incorporate and cover. Let chill in the refrigerator for 1 hour before serving.

Exchanges/Choices
1 1/2 Fruit
2 1/2 Fat

Basic Nutritional Values
Calories 210
  Calories from Fat 125
Total Fat 14 g
  Saturated Fat 1.2 g
  Trans Fat 0 g
Cholesterol 0 mg
Sodium 0 mg
Total Carbohydrate 24 g
  Dietary Fiber 4 g
  Sugars 17 g
Protein 2 g

TOMATO AND FETA SALAD

SERVES 4
SERVING SIZE: 1/4 RECIPE

1	LB TOMATOES, MEDIUM DICE
1/4	CUP REDUCED-FAT FETA CHEESE
1	TBSP EXTRA-VIRGIN OLIVE OIL
1/4	CUP BALSAMIC VINEGAR
1	TBSP MINCED GARLIC
10	BASIL LEAVES, CHIFFONADE

In a medium bowl, combine all ingredients and toss gently. You can serve immediately or let it marinate in the refrigerator.

Exchanges/Choices
1 Vegetable
1 Fat

Basic Nutritional Values
Calories 80
  Calories from Fat 40
Total Fat 4.5 g
  Saturated Fat 1.2 g
  Trans Fat 0 g
Cholesterol 0 mg
Sodium 125 mg
Total Carbohydrate 8 g
  Dietary Fiber 1 g
  Sugars 5 g
Protein 3 g

CHILLED ORECCHIETTE PASTA WITH SPINACH AND FETA CHEESE

1	TBSP MINCED GARLIC
2	TBSP BALSAMIC VINEGAR
1/4	CUP EXTRA-VIRGIN OLIVE OIL
2	CUPS COOKED ORECCHIETTE PASTA
1/2	CUP RED ONIONS, SMALL DICE
1/2	CUP RED PEPPER, SMALL DICE
1/4	CUP CHOPPED OLIVES
6	OZ FAT-FREE FETA, CRUMBLED
1	CUP FRESH SPINACH, CHIFFONADE
	DASH SALT AND PEPPER

SERVES 4
SERVING SIZE: 1/2 CUP PASTA

1. In a medium bowl, combine garlic, balsamic vinegar, and olive oil, whisking until blended.

2. In a separate large bowl, combine all ingredients until evenly coated. Refrigerate for 2 hours and serve chilled.

Exchanges/Choices
2 Starch
1 Lean Meat
2 Fat

Basic Nutritional Values
Calories 305
  Calories from Fat 135
Total Fat 15 g
  Saturated Fat 2.1 g
  Trans Fat 0 g
Cholesterol 0 mg
Sodium 740 mg
Total Carbohydrate 30 g
  Dietary Fiber 2 g
  Sugars 5 g
Protein 13 g

This recipe is high in sodium.

Tips for the Kitchen

Orecchiette pasta is shaped like a tortoise shell and about the size of a penny. It is available in most markets. You can substitute any bite-size pasta, if you prefer.

Penne a la Vodka

SERVES 4
SERVING SIZE: 1/4 RECIPE

Exchanges/Choices
2 Starch
1 Fat

Basic Nutritional Values

Calories 205
  Calories from Fat 55
Total Fat 6 g
  Saturated Fat 0.9 g
  Trans Fat 0 g
Cholesterol 0 mg
Sodium 235 mg
Total Carbohydrate 28 g
  Dietary Fiber 2 g
  Sugars 5 g
Protein 5 g

1	TBSP OLIVE OIL
1	TBSP MINCED GARLIC
1/4	CUP VODKA
2	CUPS MARINARA SAUCE (SEE RECIPE ON P. 18)
1/2	CUP FAT-FREE HALF & HALF
2	CUPS COOKED PENNE PASTA
1	TSP SALT (OPTIONAL)
1/2	TSP BLACK PEPPER (OPTIONAL)
2	TBSP FRESH BASIL, CHIFFONADE

1. Heat a large pot and add olive oil and garlic. Remove from heat. Add vodka and marinara sauce; bring to a simmer. Add half & half and bring to a simmer again.

2. In a separate pot, bring 2 cups of water to a boil and reheat cooked pasta. When pasta is finished, drain it and add it to the pot with the sauce. Stir to coat pasta with sauce. Remove from heat, season with salt and pepper, if desired, and finish with fresh basil. Serve hot.

CHICKEN BREAST WITH TOMATO AND HERBS

4	SKINLESS CHICKEN BREASTS (ABOUT 1 LB TOTAL)
3	TBSP OLIVE OIL
1/2	TSP SALT
1	TSP PAPRIKA
1/4	CUP SHALLOTS
1	CUP TOMATOES, DICED
1	CUP CHICKEN STOCK (SEE RECIPE ON P. 24)
2	TSP MINCED FRESH OREGANO
1	TBSP MINCED FRESH PARSLEY

SERVES 4
SERVING SIZE: 1 BREAST

Exchanges/Choices
4 Lean Meat
1 1/2 Fat

Basic Nutritional Values
Calories 235
  Calories from Fat 115
Total Fat 13 g
  Saturated Fat 2.2 g
  Trans Fat 0 g
Cholesterol 65 mg
Sodium 355 mg
Total Carbohydrate 4 g
  Dietary Fiber 1 g
  Sugars 2 g
Protein 25 g

1. In a medium bowl, combine chicken, 1 Tbsp olive oil, salt, and paprika and incorporate. Cover and refrigerate for 1 hour.

2. Preheat a large pan and add 1 Tbsp olive oil. Add chicken breasts to pan and sear until golden in color. Turn over and repeat.

3. When both sides are seared, remove chicken from pan and place on a baking sheet. Place into a preheated 375°F oven and cook until temperature is 160°F, about 15–20 minutes.

4. Prepare the sauce. Add 1 Tbsp olive oil to a preheated pan and add shallots. Sauté shallots, stirring until lightly browned. Add diced tomatoes and cook for just a few minutes, enough time for the tomatoes to finish cooking. When tomatoes are done, add stock and bring to a low simmer. Season with oregano and parsley. Keep warm until chicken is fully cooked, and then add the chicken to the sauce and continue to simmer while basting chicken with the sauce. Serve when sauce is reduced and slightly thickened.

CAJUN CAT

SERVES 4
SERVING SIZE: 1 FILLET

1/2	CUP FLOUR
1	TSP SALT
1	TBSP DRIED OREGANO
1	TBSP DRIED THYME LEAVES
1	TBSP PAPRIKA
1	TBSP ONION POWDER
1/2	TSP FRESH GROUND BLACK PEPPER
1/2	TSP CAYENNE PEPPER
1	TBSP OLIVE OIL
4	CATFISH FILLETS (ABOUT 4 OZ EACH)

1. Mix flour, salt, and spices in a bowl and lightly coat catfish fillets.

2. In a large skillet, heat the olive oil. Add catfish and sear until golden brown. Flip and repeat on each side for each fillet. Cook until fish is firm and fully cooked.

Exchanges/Choices
1 Starch
3 Lean Meat
1 Fat

Basic Nutritional Values
Calories 260
  Calories from Fat 110
Total Fat 12 g
  Saturated Fat 2.4 g
  Trans Fat 0 g
Cholesterol 65 mg
Sodium 665 mg
Total Carbohydrate 16 g
  Dietary Fiber 2 g
  Sugars 2 g
Protein 21 g

This recipe is
high in sodium.

Baked
Chicken Enchiladas

8	FLOUR TORTILLAS
1	LB SHREDDED COOKED CHICKEN
1/2	CUP ONIONS, SMALL DICE
1/4	CUP CHILIES, SMALL DICE
12	OZ FAT-FREE MILD CHEDDAR CHEESE
	COOKING SPRAY
1	CUP ENCHILADA SAUCE (SEE RECIPE ON P. 20)

SERVES 8
SERVING SIZE: 1 ENCHILADA

1. Evenly fill each tortilla with cooked chicken, onions, and chilies. Sprinkle cheese on top and roll up each tortilla.

2. Spray a baking dish with cooking spray and place stuffed tortillas into dish. Cover with enchilada sauce; cover dish. Bake in a preheated 375°F oven until bubbling around the edges, about 25–30 minutes. Remove cover and top with any remaining cheese; allow cheese to melt and then serve hot.

Exchanges/Choices
1 Starch
4 Lean Meat

Basic Nutritional Values
Calories 285
  Calories from Fat 65
Total Fat 7 g
  Saturated Fat 1.8 g
  Trans Fat 0 g
Cholesterol 60 mg
Sodium 735 mg
Total Carbohydrate 19 g
  Dietary Fiber 1 g
  Sugars 2 g
Protein 33 g

This recipe is
high in sodium.

GRILLED SKIRT STEAK

SERVES 4
SERVING SIZE: 1 STEAK

4	BEEF SKIRT STEAKS (4 OZ EACH)
2	CLOVES GARLIC, MINCED
1/4	CUP TERIYAKI SAUCE
2	TBSP RICE VINEGAR
1	TBSP BROWN SUGAR
1/2	SPRIG FRESH ROSEMARY

Exchanges/Choices
1/2 Carbohydrate
3 Lean Meat

Basic Nutritional Values
Calories 180
  Calories from Fat 55
Total Fat 6 g
  Saturated Fat 2.5 g
  Trans Fat 0 g
Cholesterol 40 mg
Sodium 370 mg
Total Carbohydrate 7 g
  Dietary Fiber 0 g
  Sugars 7 g
Protein 24 g

1. Remove any excess fat or sinew from steaks. Combine all other ingredients and marinate steaks overnight in the refrigerator.

2. Grill steaks over medium-high heat. Cook to desired doneness.

Mexican-Style Shrimp Cocktail, p. 125

Poached Salmon with Leeks, p. 111

Cajun Lemon Shrimp, p. 83
Dirty Rice, p. 139

Mango and Blueberry Crepes, p. 143

Shrimp and Sweet Pea Risotto, p. 116

Roast Leg of Lamb, p. 172

Baked Salmon with Mango Vinaigrette, p. 87
Peas with Caramelized Pearl Onions, p. 163

Chocolate Berry Purses, p. 119
Pumpkin Bites, 187

DIRTY RICE

1	TBSP OLIVE OIL
1/2	CUP ONIONS, SMALL DICE
1	TSP CRUSHED OREGANO
1	TSP MINCED FRESH THYME
2	TSP PAPRIKA
1/2	TSP CAYENNE PEPPER
1	CUP BROWN RICE
2 1/2	CUPS HOT CHICKEN STOCK (SEE RECIPE ON P. 24)

SERVES 6
SERVING SIZE: 1/6 RECIPE

Heat a pan and add olive oil and onions. Sweat the onions; then add spices and continue to stir. Add rice and chicken stock; stir again to incorporate. Cover rice and lower heat until rice is fluffy and tender. Serve hot.

Exchanges/Choices
2 Starch

Basic Nutritional Values
Calories 145
  Calories from Fat 30
Total Fat 3.5 g
  Saturated Fat 0.5 g
  Trans Fat 0 g
Cholesterol 0 mg
Sodium 10 mg
Total Carbohydrate 26 g
  Dietary Fiber 2 g
  Sugars 1 g
Protein 3 g

SWEET
POTATO PANCAKES

SERVES 6
SERVING SIZE: 1/6 RECIPE

Exchanges/Choices
2 Starch
1 Fat

Basic Nutritional Values
Calories 205
  Calories from Fat 40
Total Fat 4.5 g
  Saturated Fat 2.1 g
  Trans Fat 0 g
Cholesterol 80 mg
Sodium 295 mg
Total Carbohydrate 32 g
  Dietary Fiber 3 g
  Sugars 10 g
Protein 9 g

4	CUPS WATER
2	MEDIUM SWEET POTATOES, PEELED AND QUARTERED
1	CUP BUCKWHEAT FLOUR, SIFTED
1	TSP BAKING POWDER
1	TBSP BROWN SUGAR
2	TSP BUTTER, MELTED
2	CUPS LOW-FAT MILK
2	EGG YOLKS
1	TSP VANILLA EXTRACT
2	EGG WHITES
1/4	CUP FAT-FREE SOUR CREAM

1. In a medium pot, bring water to a boil. Place the sweet potatoes in the pot and simmer until soft, about 20–25 minutes. Remove potatoes from the water and let cool slightly.

2. Mash the potatoes in a large bowl and add the flour, baking powder, and brown sugar. Mix well. Pour in the melted butter, milk, egg yolks, and vanilla and mix to incorporate.

3. In a separate bowl, whisk the egg whites until stiff and then fold into the potato batter.

4. Prepare sweet potato pancakes on a hot skillet. Serve with a small dollop of sour cream.

CHILLED BROCCOLI WITH TOASTED ALMONDS

1	TSP SALT
1	LB BROCCOLI FLORETS
1/4	CUP ALMONDS, TOASTED
1	TBSP MINCED FRESH TARRAGON
1/4	CUP GREEN BELL PEPPER, SMALL DICE
	ASIAN-STYLE VINAIGRETTE (SEE RECIPE ON P. 27)

SERVES 6
SERVING SIZE: 1/6 RECIPE

1. Bring 1 quart of water to a boil in a medium pot. Add salt, and then add broccoli. Cook until tender, about 2–4 minutes.

2. Remove broccoli from water and place in a cold water bath to stop the cooking process. Thoroughly drain and place broccoli in a medium bowl. Add the remaining ingredients and toss gently, making sure salad is thoroughly coated with the vinaigrette. Chill for 1 hour and serve.

Exchanges/Choices
----
1 Vegetable
3 1/2 Fat

Basic Nutritional Values

Calories 185
  Calories from Fat 155
Total Fat 17 g
  Saturated Fat 1.4 g
  Trans Fat 0 g
Cholesterol 0 mg
Sodium 140 mg
Total Carbohydrate 6 g
  Dietary Fiber 3 g
  Sugars 2 g
Protein 4 g

GRILLED PATTYPAN SKEWERS

SERVES 4
SERVING SIZE: 8 PIECES

2	TBSP OLIVE OIL
1	TBSP SHERRY VINEGAR
1	TSP MINCED CHIVES
	PEPPER, TO TASTE
16	PATTYPAN SQUASH, CUT IN HALF

Exchanges/Choices
2 Vegetable
1 1/2 Fat

Basic Nutritional Values
Calories 100
  Calories from Fat 65
Total Fat 7 g
  Saturated Fat 0.9 g
  Trans Fat 0 g
Cholesterol 0 mg
Sodium 0 mg
Total Carbohydrate 8 g
  Dietary Fiber 3 g
  Sugars 4 g
Protein 2 g

1. Combine olive oil, sherry vinegar, chives, and pepper. If you are using wooden skewers, soak them in water beforehand to prevent burning.

2. Wash and pat dry pattypan squash. Remove stems and slice in half. Toss squash in oil and vinegar mixture. Using metal or wooden skewers, evenly arrange the squash halves, and grill until squash has grill marks and is cooked on both sides.

Mango and Blueberry Crepes

1	CUP WHOLE-WHEAT FLOUR
	PINCH SALT
2	LARGE EGGS
1	CUP LOW-FAT MILK, COLD
	NONSTICK COOKING SPRAY
1	PINT BLUEBERRIES, WASHED AND DRIED
1	CUP RIPE MANGO, PEELED, SMALL DICE
12	OZ FAT-FREE CREAM CHEESE
1	TBSP SUGAR
4	SPRIGS FRESH MINT

SERVES 12
SERVING SIZE: 2 CREPES

Exchanges/Choices
1/2 Starch
1/2 Fruit
1/2 Fat-Free Milk

Basic Nutritional Values
Calories 110
  Calories from Fat 15
Total Fat 1.5 g
  Saturated Fat 0.4 g
  Trans Fat 0 g
Cholesterol 40 mg
Sodium 225 mg
Total Carbohydrate 17 g
  Dietary Fiber 2 g
  Sugars 8 g
Protein 7 g

1. In a medium bowl, sift the flour and add salt.

2. In a separate bowl, beat together eggs and milk. Slowly pour wet ingredients into flour and salt, whisking until smooth and without lumps.

3. Heat a small crepe pan over medium-high heat. Spray the pan with nonstick cooking spray. Pour 1/8 cup of the crepe mixture into the pan. Lift and roll pan so the bottom of the pan is coated with a thin layer of batter. As the sides lift around the batter, lightly tap pan to dislodge the bottom of the crepe and turn over. Remove the crepe from the pan and keep warm. Continue process to cook the remaining crepes, spraying pan as needed.

4. Place blueberries in a bowl. Add diced mango, cream cheese, and sugar; gently fold to incorporate. Place about 2 Tbsp of fruit filling into each crepe and fold over. Place crepes in a baking dish and bake at 375°F for 15 minutes. Remove from oven and garnish with fresh mint. Serve immediately.

Tips for the Kitchen

This recipe makes about 24 crepes. Extra crepes can be double wrapped in plastic wrap and frozen for up to 3 weeks.

THREE MELONS WITH MIDORI

1/2	CANTALOUPE, SEEDED
1/2	CASABA MELON, SEEDED
1/2	HONEYDEW MELON, SEEDED
1	TBSP FRESH MINT, CHIFFONADE
1/4	CUP MIDORI LIQUEUR

SERVES 8
SERVING SIZE: 1/8 RECIPE

Exchanges/Choices
1 Carbohydrate

Basic Nutritional Values
Calories 80
  Calories from Fat 0
Total Fat 0 g
  Saturated Fat 0.1 g
  Trans Fat 0 g
Cholesterol 0 mg
Sodium 25 mg
Total Carbohydrate 17 g
  Dietary Fiber 2 g
  Sugars 16 g
Protein 2 g

1. Using a large melon baller, scoop out the cantaloupe half and place the melon balls in a bowl.

2. Next, using a medium melon baller, repeat the procedure with the casaba.

3. Using a small melon baller, repeat the procedure with the honeydew.

4. Add the mint and liqueur to the bowl of melon balls. Toss gently.

5. Chill the mixture in the refrigerator before serving.

Tips for the Kitchen
You will need three different sized melon ballers for this recipe. If you don't have those, you can dice the melon into three different sizes.

SEPTEMBER
&
OCTOBER

Where Is the Nearest Farm?

THIS IS a great time of year for me. The air is cooler and the days are shorter. We begin to pull out the sweaters and jackets. In the kitchen, we begin to head toward home-style or comfort foods. The lighter summer fares transition to slower cooking methods and our meals take on more flavor. Take, for example, my Tomato Soup with Smoked Poblano and Roasted Vegetables on page 150. It's a simple soup to prepare, but by adding a little twist and some complexity with that smoked poblano, you add some serious wow in your dish. A simple tomato soup takes on an entirely new dimension. Adding the roasted vegetables delivers more complexity and adds a textural turn that will leave you ready to start cooking another pot!

Another great recipe for this time of year is my Steamed Cauliflower with Tarragon on page 161. Growing up on Long Island, my family would drive out east to the farms and would get the freshest cauliflower and Brussels sprouts. Not only was it an all-day adventure, but we also felt more connected to where we are from and to the foods that come with the seasons. This recipe uses a steaming method that retains the essence of the cauliflower. The fresh tarragon adds a subtle flavor change that I hope you will enjoy.

What would October be without pumpkins on the menu! Try the Pumpkin Polenta with Cinnamon Whipped Topping on page 164. The addition of pumpkin puree to this classic and simple preparation elevates and invigorates the taste buds. You can serve this dish warm or chilled; either way, children and adults will enjoy making and eating this great dessert.

Whether it's soups, salads, stuffed pork chops, or a Warm Orange Rice Pudding (on page 166), these recipes will warm the body and comfort the soul. Enjoy the season and all the flavors that it has to offer. Lastly, go out to a local farm and experience the best of what your region has to offer. You just might meet the farmer who grew the food on your dinner table.

CHILLED BLACK BEAN AND ROASTED CORN SALSA

2	EARS ROASTED CORN
	ZEST AND JUICE OF 2 LIMES
1/2	CUP OLIVE OIL
3	CLOVES GARLIC, MINCED
1/4	CUP CHOPPED CILANTRO
2	TSP MINCED JALAPEÑO
2	CUPS COOKED BLACK BEANS
1	CUP TOMATOES, MEDIUM DICE
1	RED PEPPER, SMALL DICE
1	AVOCADO, MEDIUM DICE
1	TSP SALT
	PINCH PEPPER

SERVES 24
SERVING SIZE: 1/4 CUP

Exchanges/Choices
1/2 Starch
1 Fat

Basic Nutritional Values
Calories 80
 Calories from Fat 55
Total Fat 6 g
 Saturated Fat 0.8 g
 Trans Fat 0 g
Cholesterol 0 mg
Sodium 100 mg
Total Carbohydrate 7 g
 Dietary Fiber 2 g
 Sugars 1 g
Protein 2 g

1. Roast the corn. Soak corn and husks in water for 10 minutes. Place whole ears on a grill and cook, turning as husk browns. Cook evenly on all sides until done, about 10–12 minutes. Cut off corn kernels and set aside.

2. In a medium bowl, combine lime zest, lime juice, olive oil, garlic, cilantro, and jalapeño to prepare a vinaigrette; set aside.

3. In a large bowl, combine the corn, beans, tomatoes, pepper, avocado, salt, and pepper. Pour vinaigrette into bowl, stir completely, and refrigerate for at least 2 hours. Serve chilled.

VEGETARIAN STUFFED PHYLLO BITES

SERVES 4
SERVING SIZE: 1/4 RECIPE

1	TSP OLIVE OIL
1	CLOVE GARLIC, MINCED
1/2	CUP ZUCCHINI, JULIENNED
1/2	CUP YELLOW SQUASH, JULIENNED
1	TSP MINCED OREGANO
12	MINI PHYLLO DOUGH SHELLS
2	TBSP GRATED ROMANO CHEESE

Exchanges/Choices
1/2 Starch
1 Fat

Basic Nutritional Values
Calories 80
  Calories from Fat 45
Total Fat 5 g
  Saturated Fat 0.8 g
  Trans Fat 0 g
Cholesterol 5 mg
Sodium 80 mg
Total Carbohydrate 7 g
  Dietary Fiber 0 g
  Sugars 1 g
Protein 2 g

1. Preheat oven to 375°F.

2. Preheat a skillet and add oil. Add garlic, zucchini, and yellow squash; sauté until tender. Remove from heat and add oregano. Allow to cool.

3. Once vegetables have cooled, spoon vegetables into phyllo shells and sprinkle with cheese. Bake until cheese melts and begins to brown slightly. Remove from oven and serve immediately.

New England Clam Chowder

2 TBSP OLIVE OIL

1 CUP CELERY, SMALL DICE

1 CUP ONIONS, SMALL DICE

1 TBSP DRIED OREGANO

2 TSP DRIED THYME

1/4 CUP FLOUR, SIFTED

2 CANS (12 OZ EACH) CHOPPED CLAMS

1 QUART CLAM JUICE OR FISH STOCK (SEE RECIPE ON P. 25)

2 MEDIUM POTATOES, MEDIUM DICE

1 CUP FAT-FREE HALF & HALF

BLACK PEPPER, TO TASTE

2 TBSP PARSLEY, FINELY CHOPPED

SERVES 8
SERVING SIZE: 1/8 RECIPE

Exchanges/Choices
1 Carbohydrate
2 Lean Meat

Basic Nutritional Values
Calories 170
  Calories from Fat 45
Total Fat 5 g
  Saturated Fat 0.9 g
  Trans Fat 0 g
Cholesterol 30 mg
Sodium 340 mg
Total Carbohydrate 19 g
  Dietary Fiber 2 g
  Sugars 5 g
Protein 13 g

In a stockpot, heat oil. Add celery and onions and sweat them, but be sure not to brown them. Add oregano and thyme; continue to cook. Add flour and stir into mixture. Add chopped clams, clam juice, and potatoes; bring to a simmer. Cook until potatoes are just tender, about 10–15 minutes. Lower heat to a slight simmer and add half & half. Season with pepper and garnish each serving bowl with fresh parsley.

Tomato Soup with Smoked Poblano and Roasted Vegetables

Serves 6
Serving size: 1/6 recipe

2 Tbsp + 3 tsp olive oil
1 Tbsp minced garlic
1 28-oz can whole peeled tomatoes
1 smoked poblano pepper
1 cup chicken stock (see recipe on p. 24)
6 oz tomato puree
Salt, to taste
Pepper, to taste
1 cup fennel, small dice
1 tsp sugar
1 cup celery root, small dice
1/2 cup carrots, small dice
2 Tbsp fresh basil, chiffonade

1. Preheat a medium pot and add 2 Tbsp olive oil. Add garlic and cook until slightly opaque (a few seconds). Then add tomatoes, smoked poblano pepper, chicken stock, and tomato puree. Bring to a simmer and then reduce to a low simmer. Simmer for about 45 minutes, until tomatoes are fully cooked and liquid is slightly reduced. Remove from heat and puree in a food processor or blender. Season with salt and pepper. Set aside.

2. In a skillet, add 1 tsp olive oil and rapidly sauté fennel. Add a pinch of salt and pepper and the sugar. Cook until fennel is caramelized, about 8–10 minutes.

3. In a second skillet, add 2 tsp olive oil and rapidly sauté celery root and carrots. Add a pinch of salt and pepper. Cook until celery root and carrots are tender and slightly browned, about 8–10 minutes.

4. Combine the cooked fennel, carrots, and celery root in a medium bowl; set aside.

5. Prepare soup for service. In individual soup bowls, evenly portion the vegetables into the center of the bowls. Then, pour the soup around the vegetables and garnish with basil chiffonade. Serve immediately.

Exchanges/Choices
3 Vegetable
1 1/2 Fat

Basic Nutritional Values
Calories 145
  Calories from Fat 80
Total Fat 9 g
  Saturated Fat 1.2 g
  Trans Fat 0 g
Cholesterol 0 mg
Sodium 355 mg
Total Carbohydrate 15 g
  Dietary Fiber 3 g
  Sugars 7 g
Protein 3 g

TOSSED MIXED GREENS WITH GRILLED CHICKEN AND GOAT CHEESE

SERVES 2
SERVING SIZE: 1/2 RECIPE

Exchanges/Choices
1/2 Carbohydrate
2 Vegetable
2 Lean Meat
2 1/2 Fat

Basic Nutritional Values
Calories 290
  Calories from Fat 135
Total Fat 15 g
  Saturated Fat 3.4 g
  Trans Fat 0 g
Cholesterol 45 mg
Sodium 370 mg
Total Carbohydrate 20 g
  Dietary Fiber 3 g
  Sugars 14 g
Protein 17 g

6	OZ MIXED GREENS
2	TBSP REDUCED BALSAMIC VINEGAR (SEE RECIPE ON P. 32)
1	TBSP EXTRA-VIRGIN OLIVE OIL
1	OZ REDUCED-FAT GOAT CHEESE
2	PLUM TOMATOES, QUARTERED
1/4	CUP CARROTS, JULIENNED
12	OLIVES
1	SIMPLE CHICKEN BREAST, SLICED (SEE RECIPE ON P. 11)

1. In a large bowl, add mixed greens, reduced balsamic vinegar, and extra-virgin olive oil. Crumble in the goat cheese and toss gently. Using a pair of tongs, remove lettuce from bowl and place onto a plate, allowing it to stand as tall as possible.

2. Add other ingredients around the salad to create a balanced and beautiful salad plate.

RARE AHI TUNA WITH NAPA CABBAGE SLAW

4	AHI TUNA FILLETS (ALSO CALLED YELLOWFIN TUNA), ABOUT 4 OZ EACH
3	OZ LIGHT SOY SAUCE
3	TBSP PLUM VINEGAR
1	TSP MINCED GARLIC
1/4	CUP ORANGE JUICE
2	TBSP RICE WINE VINEGAR
1	TBSP DIJON MUSTARD
2	TSP SESAME OIL
1	TBSP CANOLA OIL
3	CUPS NAPA CABBAGE, SHREDDED
1/4	CUP CHIVES, CUT INTO 1-INCH SPRIGS

Exchanges/Choices

1 Vegetable
4 Lean Meat
1 Fat

Basic Nutritional Values

Calories 240
  Calories from Fat 100
Total Fat 11 g
  Saturated Fat 2 g
  Trans Fat 0 g
Cholesterol 40 mg
Sodium 330 mg
Total Carbohydrate 6 g
  Dietary Fiber 1 g
  Sugars 4 g
Protein 27 g

1. Place tuna in a bowl and add soy sauce, plum vinegar, and garlic. Allow to marinate for 10 minutes.

2. Sear the tuna fillets in a nonstick pan. Tuna can be cooked however you desire, but rare is generally preferred.

3. In a separate bowl, combine the orange juice, vinegar, and Dijon mustard. In a slow stream, whisk in the sesame oil and then the canola oil.

4. In another larger bowl, mix the cabbage and chives. Pour the slaw dressing over the cabbage and chives, combine thoroughly, and set aside.

5. Portion slaw evenly onto serving plates and place tuna fillets on top of beds of slaw. Serve immediately.

KUNG PAO-STYLE CHICKEN

SERVES 4
SERVING SIZE: 1/4 RECIPE

1	LB BONELESS, SKINLESS CHICKEN BREASTS, CUT INTO THIN STRIPS
2	TSP SESAME OIL
2	TBSP LIGHT SOY SAUCE
1	TBSP MINCED FRESH GINGER
1	TBSP MINCED GARLIC
1	TBSP CANOLA OIL
1/2	CUP CHOPPED SCALLIONS
1/3	CUP UNSALTED, ROASTED PEANUTS
4	DRIED CHILI PEPPERS
1/4	CUP DRY SHERRY
2	TBSP HOISIN SAUCE
1/2	CUP CHICKEN STOCK (SEE RECIPE ON P. 24)
2	TBSP CORNSTARCH
2	TBSP COLD WATER
2	CUPS COOKED WHITE RICE

Exchanges/Choices
2 Starch
4 Lean Meat
1 1/2 Fat

Basic Nutritional Values
Calories 410
  Calories from Fat 135
Total Fat 15 g
  Saturated Fat 2.3 g
  Trans Fat 0 g
Cholesterol 65 mg
Sodium 455 mg
Total Carbohydrate 34 g
  Dietary Fiber 2 g
  Sugars 4 g
Protein 31 g

1. Marinate the chicken in sesame oil, soy sauce, ginger, and garlic overnight.

2. In a wok or large skillet, heat canola oil and cook chicken. Once chicken is done, remove it from the wok and set aside.

3. Add scallions, peanuts, and dried chilies to the wok and quickly cook until scallions are wilted. Deglaze with dry sherry and then heat until liquid is reduced by half. Add hoisin sauce and chicken stock.

4. Combine cornstarch with cold water; add to wok and rapidly stir to combine until a smooth sauce is made. Add cooked chicken to wok, coat chicken with sauce, and serve over 1/2 cup rice.

VEGETABLE LO MEIN

2 TBSP SESAME OIL

1 TBSP MINCED FRESH GINGER

1 TBSP MINCED GARLIC

1/2 CUP SCALLIONS, SMALL DICE

1 HEAD BOK CHOY, WASHED AND THINLY SLICED

8 OZ SNOW PEAS

4 OZ SHREDDED CARROTS

2 TBSP SZECHWAN CHILI SAUCE

1/4 CUP LIGHT SOY SAUCE

3/4 CUP BROWN SAUCE (SEE RECIPE ON P. 22)

1 QUART WATER

1 LB COOKED WHOLE-WHEAT NOODLES

SERVES 4
SERVING SIZE: 1/4 RECIPE

1. Preheat a stockpot and add sesame oil. Add ginger, garlic, and scallions; stir quickly. Add bok choy and continue stirring to cook evenly. Once bok choy is wilted, add snow peas and carrots; continue to stir and cook. Add chili sauce, light soy sauce, and brown sauce.

2. In a separate pot, bring water to a boil and add cooked pasta to reheat. Drain pasta and combine with vegetable mixture. Gently fold to evenly coat. Serve immediately.

Exchanges/Choices
2 1/2 Starch
2 Vegetable
1 1/2 Fat

Basic Nutritional Values
Calories 310
  Calories from Fat 70
Total Fat 8 g
  Saturated Fat 1.3 g
  Trans Fat 0 g
Cholesterol 0 mg
Sodium 805 mg
Total Carbohydrate 52 g
  Dietary Fiber 10 g
  Sugars 8 g
Protein 14 g

This recipe is
high in sodium.

Pan-Seared Catfish with Light Cream Sauce

Serves 4
Serving size: 1 fillet

Exchanges/Choices
1/2 Starch
5 Lean Meat
1 Fat

Basic Nutritional Values
Calories 305
  Calories from Fat 135
Total Fat 15 g
  Saturated Fat 3.3 g
  Trans Fat 0 g
Cholesterol 100 mg
Sodium 155 mg
Total Carbohydrate 8 g
  Dietary Fiber 0 g
  Sugars 2 g
Protein 30 g

4	CATFISH FILLETS (6 OZ EACH)
	PINCH SALT
	PINCH BLACK PEPPER
2	TBSP FLOUR, SIFTED
2	TSP OLIVE OIL

Sauce

1	TBSP MINCED SHALLOTS
1/2	CUP DRY WHITE WINE
1	CUP FISH STOCK (SEE RECIPE ON P. 25)
1/2	CUP FAT-FREE HALF & HALF
1	TBSP CORNSTARCH
2	TSP MINCED THYME
1	TBSP CHOPPED SCALLIONS

1. Place the catfish on a flat surface. Season with salt and pepper and then dredge in sifted flour.

2. Preheat a sauté pan over medium-high heat; add olive oil. Place fillets carefully in pan and cook until golden brown. Turn over and repeat until fish is cooked. Remove fish from pan.

3. Add shallots to pan and sweat them. Add white wine to deglaze; reduce until almost dry. Add fish stock and half & half; bring to a simmer. Add a small amount of water to the cornstarch to make slurry and whisk into sauce to thicken. Add thyme and finish with scallions. Pour sauce over fish and serve.

POACHED SALMON WITH MARINARA SAUCE

2 CUPS WHITE WINE

2 CUPS WATER

1 MEDIUM ONION, CLEANED AND CUT IN QUARTERS

4 SPRIGS FRESH THYME

1/2 TSP WHOLE PEPPERCORNS

2 BAY LEAVES

1 LEMON WEDGE, SEEDS REMOVED

4 SALMON FILLETS (4 OZ EACH)

1 TBSP OLIVE OIL

1 TBSP MINCED GARLIC

2 CUPS MARINARA SAUCE (SEE RECIPE ON P. 18)

1 TSP MINCED OREGANO

PINCH FRESH GROUND BLACK PEPPER

SERVES 4
SERVING SIZE: 1 FILLET

Exchanges/Choices
1/2 Starch
3 Lean Meat
1 1/2 Fat

Basic Nutritional Values
Calories 245
Calories from Fat 100
Total Fat 11 g
Saturated Fat 2.1 g
Trans Fat 0 g
Cholesterol 50 mg
Sodium 255 mg
Total Carbohydrate 6 g
Dietary Fiber 2 g
Sugars 3 g
Protein 26 g

1. Combine the white wine, water, onion, thyme, peppercorns, bay leaf, and lemon wedge, and bring to a simmer in a large shallow pan.

2. Place salmon fillets into poaching liquid, making sure that the fillets are submerged. Bring liquid back to a simmer; cook for another 10 minutes or until done. Remove fillets from poaching liquid and set aside, covered. Strain liquid and reserve.

3. In a medium pan, heat the olive oil. Add garlic and cook until it turns opaque. Immediately add marinara sauce and bring to a simmer. Add 1 cup reserved poaching liquid; simmer for 10 minutes. Using a food processor, blend until smooth.

4. Return blended marinara sauce to the saucepan. Add oregano and season with pepper. Add 1/2 cup reserved poaching liquid; bring back to a simmer for 1–2 minutes and then reserve until needed.

5. Pour marinara sauce into four serving bowls. Place poached salmon on top and serve.

PORK CHOPS STUFFED WITH CARAMELIZED FENNEL IN SHIITAKE MUSHROOM SAUCE

SERVES 4
SERVING SIZE: 1 PORK CHOP

1	FENNEL BULB
1 Tbsp + 3	TSP OLIVE OIL
1 1/2	TSP SALT
1/2	TSP PEPPER
1	Tbsp SUGAR
4	BONELESS PORK CHOPS (6 OZ EACH), TRIMMED OF FAT
1/4	CUP SHALLOTS, SMALL DICE
1/2	LB SHIITAKE MUSHROOMS, STEMS REMOVED AND SLICED
1/4	CUP WHITE WINE
1	CUP CHICKEN STOCK (SEE RECIPE ON P. 24)
1/2	CUP BROWN SAUCE (SEE RECIPE ON P. 22)
1	Tbsp FRESH PARSLEY

1. Slice the fennel into thin strips. In a large nonstick skillet, preheat 1 Tbsp olive oil. Cook fennel until brown. Season with 1 tsp salt, 1/2 tsp pepper, and sugar. Remove from heat and set aside.

2. Remove any excess fat from the pork chops. Butterfly the chops. Then, evenly distribute fennel on top of each chop. Fold over and season with 1/2 tsp salt and a pinch of pepper. (If needed, tie the chops closed with butcher's twine.)

3. Heat another skillet and add 1 tsp olive oil. Sear chops and remove from pan. Transfer to a baking sheet and bake at 375°F. Bake until chops reach an internal temperature of 165°F, about 20 minutes.

4. While chops are cooking, reheat the skillet used for searing the chops. Add 2 tsp olive oil and shallots. Stir shallots and sweat. Add shiitake mushrooms; continue to cook. Deglaze pan with wine; then add chicken stock and brown sauce. Bring to a simmer and then reduce heat.

5. When chops are fully cooked, transfer chops to pan and baste with sauce. Place on serving dishes and garnish with fresh parsley.

Exchanges/Choices
1/2 Carbohydrate
1 Vegetable
5 Lean Meat
2 Fat

Basic Nutritional Values
Calories 360
  Calories from Fat 160
Total Fat 18 g
  Saturated Fat 4.7 g
  Trans Fat 0 g
Cholesterol 90 mg
Sodium 985 mg
Total Carbohydrate 14 g
  Dietary Fiber 3 g
  Sugars 6 g
Protein 35 g

This recipe is
high in sodium.

GRILLED DIJON AND BALSAMIC CHICKEN

SERVES 4
SERVING SIZE: 1 BREAST

Exchanges/Choices
1/2 Carbohydrate
3 Lean Meat
1/2 Fat

Basic Nutritional Values
Calories 185
  Calories from Fat 65
Total Fat 7 g
  Saturated Fat 1.3 g
  Trans Fat 0 g
Cholesterol 65 mg
Sodium 420 mg
Total Carbohydrate 5 g
  Dietary Fiber 1 g
  Sugars 3 g
Protein 25 g

1/4 CUP DIJON MUSTARD
1 TBSP REDUCED BALSAMIC VINEGAR (SEE RECIPE ON P. 32)
JUICE OF 1/2 LIME
1 TBSP OLIVE OIL
10 SPRIGS FRESH THYME
4 BONELESS, SKINLESS CHICKEN BREASTS (ABOUT 1 LB TOTAL)

1. Combine Dijon mustard, balsamic vinegar, lime juice, olive oil, and fresh thyme. Add chicken breasts and marinate overnight.

2. Preheat a grill and grill over medium heat. Be careful not to scorch the chicken. Cook chicken until it reaches an internal temperature of 165°F.

STEAMED CAULIFLOWER WITH TARRAGON

1	CAULIFLOWER HEAD
1 1/2	CUPS WATER
1	TBSP BUTTER
1	TBSP MINCED FRESH TARRAGON
1/4	TSP WHITE PEPPER

SERVES 6
SERVING SIZE: 1/6 RECIPE

1. Remove any leaves from the cauliflower head and discard. Rinse with cold water and set aside.

2. In a large pot, bring water and butter to a simmer. Place the head of cauliflower in the pot. Sprinkle with tarragon and white pepper. Cover.

3. Steam the cauliflower for 10–15 minutes or until tender. (A toothpick should go in easily.)

4. Remove the cauliflower from the pot and place in a serving dish. Simmer liquid in pot until liquid has been reduced to one-third of the original volume.

5. Pour the reduced cooking liquid over the cauliflower head and serve immediately.

Exchanges/Choices
1 Vegetable
1/2 Fat

Basic Nutritional Values
Calories 40
  Calories from Fat 20
Total Fat 2 g
  Saturated Fat 1.2 g
  Trans Fat 0 g
Cholesterol 5 mg
Sodium 45 mg
Total Carbohydrate 5 g
  Dietary Fiber 2 g
  Sugars 2 g
Protein 2 g

MASHED POTATOES AND PARSNIPS

SERVES 6
SERVING SIZE: 1/6 RECIPE

2	QUARTS WATER
12	OZ POTATOES, PEELED AND QUARTERED
8	OZ PARSNIPS, PEELED, CENTER CUT OUT, LARGE DICE
1	TSP SALT
	WHITE PEPPER, TO TASTE
1/2	TSP NUTMEG
1	CUP WARM LOW-FAT MILK

Exchanges/Choices
1 Starch

Basic Nutritional Values
Calories 85
  Calories from Fat 5
Total Fat 0.5 g
  Saturated Fat 0.3 g
  Trans Fat 0 g
Cholesterol 5 mg
Sodium 115 mg
Total Carbohydrate 17 g
  Dietary Fiber 2 g
  Sugars 4 g
Protein 3 g

1. Bring water to a boil and add potatoes and parsnips. Simmer for 20 minutes or until potatoes and parsnips are fork tender. Drain water.

2. Using a potato ricer or food mill, process the potatoes and parsnips. Place puree back into pot and fold in the rest of the ingredients. Serve immediately.

PEAS WITH CARAMELIZED PEARL ONIONS

2   TSP OLIVE OIL

6   OZ PEARL ONIONS, SKIN REMOVED

2   TBSP FORTIFIED CHICKEN STOCK (SEE
    RECIPE ON P. 24)

1/2   TSP SALT
    PINCH BLACK PEPPER

1   CUP WATER

8   OZ PEAS, FRESH OR FROZEN

SERVES 4
SERVING SIZE: 1/4 RECIPE

1. Preheat a skillet over medium-high heat. Add the olive oil and then the onions. Brown the onions on all sides.

2. Add the chicken stock, salt, and pepper. Allow the liquid to absorb into the onions. Continue cooking until almost all of the liquid is absorbed. Set aside.

3. In a medium pot, bring the water to a boil. Add the peas. Simmer uncovered for 3–5 minutes or until the peas are tender.

4. Drain the peas and combine with the reserved caramelized onions. Serve immediately.

Exchanges/Choices
1 Starch

Basic Nutritional Values
Calories 80
  Calories from Fat 20
Total Fat 2.5 g
  Saturated Fat 0.3 g
  Trans Fat 0 g
Cholesterol 0 mg
Sodium 105 mg
Total Carbohydrate 12 g
  Dietary Fiber 3 g
  Sugars 5 g
Protein 3 g

PUMPKIN POLENTA WITH CINNAMON WHIPPED TOPPING

SERVES 6
SERVING SIZE: 1/6 RECIPE

Exchanges/Choices
2 1/2 Carbohydrate

Basic Nutritional Values
Calories 190
  Calories from Fat 15
Total Fat 1.5 g
  Saturated Fat 0.7 g
  Trans Fat 0 g
Cholesterol 5 mg
Sodium 60 mg
Total Carbohydrate 37 g
  Dietary Fiber 3 g
  Sugars 10 g
Protein 5 g

1	CUP WATER
2	CUPS LOW-FAT MILK
3/4	CUP PUMPKIN PUREE
1	TBSP SUGAR
1/2	TSP NUTMEG
1	TSP CINNAMON
1	CUP CORNMEAL, COARSE YELLOW
6	OZ FAT-FREE WHIPPED TOPPING (OPTIONAL)
1/2	TSP CINNAMON (OPTIONAL)

1. In a medium pot, bring the water, milk, and pumpkin puree to a simmer. Add the sugar, nutmeg, and cinnamon. Slowly add the cornmeal in an even pour, whisking to incorporate. Reduce heat to a low simmer and cook, stirring as needed, until tender and thickened. If polenta thickens too much, add a small amount of low-fat milk to get a smooth creamy texture.

2. Pour the mixture evenly into six soufflé dishes. If desired, garnish with a small dollop of whipped topping and a pinch of cinnamon. Can be served immediately or allowed to cool and served later.

PEAR AND WALNUT MIX

1	BOSC PEAR, CORED AND FINELY DICED
1	BARTLETT PEAR, CORED AND FINELY DICED
1	ANJOU PEAR, CORED AND FINELY DICED
1	CUP WALNUTS, COARSELY CHOPPED
2	TBSP HONEY
1/2	TSP GROUND CINNAMON
2	TSP MINCED FRESH MINT
1	TSP VANILLA EXTRACT

SERVES 16
SERVING SIZE: 1/4 CUP

Combine all ingredients in a medium bowl. This mix can be used as a cake topping or as an addition to fresh fruit.

Exchanges/Choices
1/2 Carbohydrate
1 Fat

Basic Nutritional Values
Calories 75
  Calories from Fat 45
Total Fat 5 g
  Saturated Fat 0.5 g
  Trans Fat 0 g
Cholesterol 0 mg
Sodium 0 mg
Total Carbohydrate 8 g
  Dietary Fiber 2 g
  Sugars 5 g
Protein 1 g

Tips for the Kitchen

The three different varieties of pears used in this recipe each impart their own unique flavor and texture. However, the recipe can be made successfully using only one type of pear.

Warm Orange Rice Pudding

Serves 4
Serving size: 1/4 recipe

1	CUP WATER
2	TSP VANILLA EXTRACT
1	TSP GROUND GINGER
2	TBSP SUGAR
1	CUP ARBORIO RICE
1	TBSP ORANGE ZEST
2	CUPS LOW-FAT MILK
1/4	CUP ORANGE SEGMENTS

Exchanges/Choices
2 1/2 Starch
1/2 Fat-Free Milk

Basic Nutritional Values
Calories 240
  Calories from Fat 15
Total Fat 1.5 g
  Saturated Fat 0.9 g
  Trans Fat 0 g
Cholesterol 10 mg
Sodium 65 mg
Total Carbohydrate 48 g
  Dietary Fiber 1 g
  Sugars 14 g
Protein 7 g

In a saucepan, bring water to a boil and add vanilla, ginger, sugar, and Arborio rice. Lower heat and allow rice to absorb liquid, stirring as needed, about 10 minutes. When most of the liquid has been absorbed, add the orange zest and 1 cup milk. Allow the rice to absorb liquid and then add the other cup of milk. Continue cooking until all liquid is absorbed and rice is fully cooked. Serve in individual bowls with an orange segment on top.

NOVEMBER & DECEMBER

THANKSGIVING TIDBITS

EVERY YEAR, people frantically run around looking for last-minute help with their Thanksgiving feasts. Here are some tips to help your meal go without hitting any hitches.

When working with raw meat, use hot soapy water to wash your hands, knives, cutting boards, and kitchen counters. Wash between uses.

Here's what the label on a turkey means:
   Fresh: chilled to 40°F, so roast within 1–2 days or it'll go bad.
   Rapidly frozen: frozen to below 32°F and then stored at 0°F or lower.
   Natural: contains no artificial or synthetic additives and has minimal processing.
   Kosher: prepared under rabbinical direction.
   Basted/self-basting: injected or marinated with liquid that raises overall weight by up to 12%.

You will get more meat per pound with a large turkey.

Remove the giblet bag before cooking.

If you like dark meat, buy two small turkeys. You will have more wings, thighs, and drumsticks, and you'll also have a shorter cooking time!

Check for doneness. Stick a meat thermometer in the thickest part of the meat without touching bone or the pan. Cook to 165°F. If the turkey is stuffed, the meat and stuffing center should be 165°F. Do not cut, pierce, or stab the meat; this will drain away the juices, resulting in tough, dry meat.

If the breast is cooking faster than the thighs, cover the breast with foil and continue cooking.

When your turkey is done cooking, let it rest for 15–20 minutes. This allows the juices to flow back into the meat.

Stuffing can be made the day before and refrigerated.

Cook stuffing to an internal temperature of 165°F in the thickest area.

Never stuff turkeys in advance. Always stuff just before cooking.

Cook cranberries until they pop. If they are overcooked, they will be mushy and taste bitter.

Almost any potato can be used for mashed potatoes. Russets make for light and fluffy mashed potatoes and Yukon Golds offer a creamy, smooth texture.

A teaspoon of lemon juice in the cooking water will keep your potatoes white.

FURTHER READING

The New Food Lover's Tiptionary: More Than 6,000 Food and Drink Tips, Secrets, Shortcuts, and Other Things Cookbooks Never Tell You, by Sharon Tyler Herbst. William Morrow Cookbooks, 2002, p. 156, 379, 382, 450, 476, 478.

10,001 Food Facts, Chefs' Secrets & Household Hints, by Dr. Myles H. Bader. Northstar Publishing, 1998, p. 276.

SWEET VIDALIA ONION TART

1	TSP OLIVE OIL
3	CUPS VIDALIA ONIONS, SLICED THIN
1/4	CUP DRY SHERRY
1	TSP SALT
1/2	TSP PEPPER
1	TSP MINCED FRESH THYME
1	LARGE EGG
1/2	CUP GRUYÈRE CHEESE, GRATED
1/4	TSP NUTMEG
8	OZ WHOLE-WHEAT PIZZA DOUGH

SERVES 12
SERVING SIZE: 1 SLICE

Exchanges/Choices
1/2 Starch
1 Vegetable
1/2 Fat

Basic Nutritional Values
Calories 95
  Calories from Fat 25
Total Fat 3 g
  Saturated Fat 1 g
  Trans Fat 0 g
Cholesterol 25 mg
Sodium 295 mg
Total Carbohydrate 12 g
  Dietary Fiber 2 g
  Sugars 2 g
Protein 4 g

1. In a large skillet, heat the olive oil and then add onions evenly. Slowly cook onions over medium-low heat until fully cooked and golden brown in color. Deglaze with sherry and reduce liquid until most of the liquid has evaporated. Season with salt, pepper, and thyme; set aside to cool.

2. In a bowl, combine egg, Gruyère cheese, and nutmeg. Add cooked onions to this egg-cheese mixture and combine.

3. Evenly roll out the pizza dough. Add the onion mixture to dough, leaving a 1-inch rim around the edge. Fold edge over and place in a preheated 425°F oven. Bake for 10 minutes, then reduce the heat to 350°F and bake for an additional 20 minutes or until crust is golden brown. Remove from oven and let it rest a few minutes before serving.

ROASTED RED PEPPER HUMMUS

SERVES 16
SERVING SIZE: 2 TBSP

1   14-OZ CAN CHICKPEAS (ALSO CALLED
     GARBANZO BEANS), RINSED
1   ROASTED RED PEPPER (SEE RECIPE ON P. 29)
1/2   CUP TAHINI (SESAME SEED PASTE)
     JUICE AND ZEST FROM 1 LEMON
2   CLOVES GARLIC
1/2   TSP CUMIN
1   TSP SALT
     PINCH PEPPER

Exchanges/Choices
1/2 Starch
1 Fat

Basic Nutritional Values
Calories 70
  Calories from Fat 40
Total Fat 4.5 g
  Saturated Fat 0.6 g
  Trans Fat 0 g
Cholesterol 0 mg
Sodium 180 mg
Total Carbohydrate 7 g
  Dietary Fiber 2 g
  Sugars 1 g
Protein 3 g

Put all ingredients in a food processor and blend until smooth.
Refrigerate for 2 hours before serving.

ROASTED EGGPLANT SOUP

COOKING SPRAY

1 1/2	LB EGGPLANT
1	TBSP OLIVE OIL
1	CUP DICED ONIONS
1	TBSP MINCED GARLIC
1	QUART CHICKEN STOCK (SEE RECIPE ON P. 24)
1	1-INCH SPRIG FRESH ROSEMARY
4	SPRIGS FRESH THYME
2	TSP GROUND CUMIN
1 1/2	CUPS FAT-FREE HALF & HALF
2	TSP SALT
1	TSP PEPPER

SERVES 8
SERVING SIZE: 1/8 RECIPE

1. Preheat oven to 350°F. Spray a baking sheet with cooking spray. Slice eggplant lengthwise and place face down on a baking sheet. Bake for 30–45 minutes, until eggplant is soft and tender. Remove eggplant from oven and allow to cool slightly. With a large spoon, scoop eggplant from skin and remove seeds.

2. Preheat a medium pot; add olive oil and onions. Sweat onions; then add garlic, chicken stock, rosemary, thyme, cumin, and eggplant. Bring to a simmer; then reduce to a low simmer. Cook for 20 minutes. Transfer mixture to a food processor and blend until smooth. Whisk in half & half and season with salt and pepper. Serve immediately.

Exchanges/Choices
1 Carbohydrate
1/2 Fat

Basic Nutritional Values
Calories 80
  Calories from Fat 25
Total Fat 3 g
  Saturated Fat 0.7 g
  Trans Fat 0 g
Cholesterol 5 mg
Sodium 635 mg
Total Carbohydrate 13 g
  Dietary Fiber 2 g
  Sugars 5 g
Protein 3 g

This recipe is
high in sodium.

ROAST LEG OF LAMB

SERVES 10
SERVING SIZE: 1/10 RECIPE

Exchanges/Choices
1 Vegetable
4 Lean Meat
1 Fat

Basic Nutritional Values
Calories 255
  Calories from Fat 110
Total Fat 12 g
  Saturated Fat 3.6 g
  Trans Fat 0 g
Cholesterol 90 mg
Sodium 555 mg
Total Carbohydrate 6 g
  Dietary Fiber 1 g
  Sugars 2 g
Protein 29 g

5	LB LEG OF LAMB, TRIMMED OF FAT
5	CLOVES GARLIC, CLEANED
2	TBSP OLIVE OIL
2	TSP SALT
1	TSP BLACK PEPPER
2	SPRIGS FRESH ROSEMARY
1	TBSP MINCED OREGANO
2	MEDIUM ONIONS, CLEANED AND CUT INTO QUARTERS
2	CARROTS, PEELED AND DICED LARGE
2	CELERY STALKS, CLEANED AND DICED LARGE

1. Trim away the excess fat on the lamb. Make five small slits in the lamb and insert the cloves of garlic. Pour olive oil over the meat, and season with salt, pepper, rosemary, and oregano. Preheat oven to 450°F.

2. In the bottom of a roasting pan, add the onions, carrots, and celery. Place lamb on the pan's metal rack. Place roasting pan in the oven and bake for 20 minutes. Then lower the temperature to 325°F and continue to roast for 25 minutes per pound (about 2 hours) or until the roast reaches an internal temperature of 145°F for medium rare or 160°F for medium.

3. Remove roast from oven and let it rest for 15 minutes. Carve and serve.

STUFFED EGGPLANT WITH ROASTED RED PEPPERS

4	EGGS
1/4	CUP LOW-FAT MILK
1/2	CUP FAT-FREE MOZZARELLA, GRATED
1 3/4	CUPS LOW-FAT RICOTTA CHEESE
1	TBSP CHOPPED FRESH PARSLEY
1	TSP SALT
1/2	TSP PEPPER
1	LARGE EGGPLANT
2	CUPS BREAD CRUMBS
2	ROASTED RED PEPPERS, JULIENNED (SEE RECIPE ON P. 29)
2	CUPS MARINARA SAUCE (SEE RECIPE ON P. 18)

SERVES 6
SERVING SIZE: 1/6 RECIPE

1. Preheat oven to 375°F.

2. Combine 3 eggs and low-fat milk; set aside.

3. In another bowl, combine mozzarella, low-fat ricotta cheese, parsley, 1 egg, salt, and pepper.

4. Peel eggplant and slice lengthwise into thin 1/4-inch strips. Dip eggplant into egg and milk mixture. Then dip eggplant strips into the bread crumbs; shake off excess. Place eggplant strips on a baking sheet.

5. Bake eggplant strips until lightly browned, about 25 minutes.

6. Place cooked eggplant flat on a work surface. Evenly portion ricotta cheese mixture over eggplant and add roasted red pepper strips on top. Roll eggplant to individual servings.

7. Pour marinara sauce into a baking dish; add rolled eggplant to dish. Bake until eggplant rolls reach an internal temperature of 160°F, about 30–40 minutes. Serve hot.

Exchanges/Choices
1 1/2 Starch
2 Vegetable
2 Lean Meat
1 Fat

Basic Nutritional Values
Calories 295
  Calories from Fat 80
Total Fat 9 g
  Saturated Fat 3.7 g
  Trans Fat 0 g
Cholesterol 130 mg
Sodium 1025 mg
Total Carbohydrate 38 g
  Dietary Fiber 6 g
  Sugars 12 g
Protein 20 g

This recipe is high in sodium.

BRAISED STUFFED CABBAGE

SERVES 8
SERVING SIZE: 1 CABBAGE ROLL

8	WHOLE CABBAGE LEAVES
3	QUARTS WATER
2 1/2	TSP SALT
1 TBSP + 2	TSP OLIVE OIL
1	ONION, SMALL DICE
8	OZ WHITE MUSHROOMS, SLICED
	PINCH PEPPER
4	OZ LEAN HAM, SMALL DICE
2	CUPS COOKED WILD RICE
3	TSP OREGANO
2	CLOVES GARLIC, MINCED
1	10-OZ CAN CRUSHED TOMATOES
1	TBSP TOMATO PASTE
1/2	TSP RED PEPPER FLAKES
1/4	CUP CHICKEN STOCK (SEE RECIPE ON P. 24)

Exchanges/Choices
1/2 Starch
1 Vegetable
1 Fat

Basic Nutritional Values
Calories 115
 Calories from Fat 35
Total Fat 4 g
 Saturated Fat 0.7 g
 Trans Fat 0 g
Cholesterol 10 mg
Sodium 475 mg
Total Carbohydrate 15 g
 Dietary Fiber 2 g
 Sugars 3 g
Protein 6 g

1. Blanch the cabbage first. Bring the water to a simmer and add 2 tsp salt. Submerge cabbage leaves in batches to ensure even cooking. Cook leaves until tender, about 1–2 minutes; quickly remove leaves and plunge them into a chilled water bath. Pat leaves dry; remove and discard thick stems.

2. In a skillet, heat 1 Tbsp olive oil and sweat the onions. Add sliced mushrooms and continue to cook until mushrooms are slightly browned. Season with 1/2 tsp salt and pepper, and then add ham. Continue to sauté for 1 minute. Remove from heat, mix with cooked wild rice and 1 tsp oregano, and set aside.

3. Portion rice stuffing evenly into each cabbage leaf and fold into a tight roll.

4. Preheat a skillet and add 2 tsp olive oil. Add garlic, crushed tomatoes, tomato paste, 2 tsp oregano, and red pepper flakes. Stir to combine ingredients. Add chicken stock and bring to a simmer. While liquid is simmering, gently add stuffed cabbage rolls, spacing them evenly apart. Reduce heat and cover. Occasionally baste the rolls. Rolls are done when they reach an internal temperature of 180°F or leaves are tender.

SHRIMP AND CLAM STEW

4 LB CLAMS

8 OZ UNPEELED SHRIMP

2 TBSP GARLIC, MINCED

1 CUP WHITE WINE

2 TBSP OLIVE OIL

1/2 CUP ONIONS, SMALL DICE

1 CUP MUSHROOMS, DICED

1 CUP MARINARA SAUCE (SEE RECIPE ON P. 18)

1 CUP FISH STOCK (SEE RECIPE ON P. 25)

2 TBSP OREGANO, MINCED

PINCH PEPPER

SERVES 4
SERVING SIZE: 1/4 RECIPE

Exchanges/Choices

2 Vegetable

3 Lean Meat

1 Fat

Basic Nutritional Values

Calories 255
  Calories from Fat 80
Total Fat 9 g
  Saturated Fat 1.3 g
  Trans Fat 0 g
Cholesterol 115 mg
Sodium 325 mg
Total Carbohydrate 11 g
  Dietary Fiber 2 g
  Sugars 6 g
Protein 27 g

1. Wash clams and place in a large stockpot. Add shrimp, garlic, and white wine. Cover. Bring to a simmer and cook clams until all are open; discard those that remain closed. Remove pot from heat and let cool slightly. Remove meat from clams and add to the shrimp and wine mixture. Set aside.

2. Preheat another large stockpot. Add olive oil, onions, and mushrooms; sauté. Add marinara sauce and fish stock and bring to a simmer. Add shrimp and clam mixture. Simmer for a few more minutes. Add oregano and season with pepper. Serve immediately.

TURKEY STEW

SERVES 4
SERVING SIZE: 1/4 RECIPE

Exchanges/Choices
1/2 Starch
1 Vegetable
5 Lean Meat
1 1/2 Fat

Basic Nutritional Values
Calories 355
  Calories from Fat 125
Total Fat 14 g
  Saturated Fat 2.3 g
  Trans Fat 0 g
Cholesterol 110 mg
Sodium 110 mg
Total Carbohydrate 15 g
  Dietary Fiber 3 g
  Sugars 2 g
Protein 41 g

2	TBSP OLIVE OIL
1/2	CUP CELERY, SMALL DICE
1/2	CUP ONIONS, SMALL DICE
1/4	CUP BABY CARROTS
1/4	CUP CORN
1	TBSP POULTRY SEASONING
1	CUP CHICKEN STOCK (SEE RECIPE ON P. 24)
1	LB COOKED TURKEY, DICED
3	CUPS TURKEY GRAVY (SEE RECIPE ON P. 17)
1/2	TSP BLACK PEPPER
2	TBSP FRESH PARSLEY, MINCED

Preheat a medium pot and add olive oil. Add celery, onions, and baby carrots; sweat them. When onions and celery begin to brown, add the corn, poultry seasoning, and chicken stock and bring to a simmer. Add diced turkey and gravy and reduce to a slow simmer. Simmer for 30 minutes or until carrots are soft and fully cooked. Season with black pepper and garnish with parsley. Serve immediately.

ROTISSERIE SMOKED TURKEY BREAST

2–3   LB HICKORY WOOD CHIPS OR SMALL CHUNKS

6   LB BONE-IN TURKEY BREAST WITH SKIN

2   TBSP CANOLA OIL

2   TSP KOSHER SALT

1/2   TSP PEPPER

2   TSP PAPRIKA

SERVES 10
SERVING SIZE: 1/10 RECIPE

1. Soak hickory wood chips in water for 30 minutes before using. Preheat grill to 350°F. Add hickory chips to the grill (in the wood smoker compartment or on the side) and allow wood to smolder. Add additional chips to maintain a light smoke.

2. Thoroughly wash turkey with cold water and pat dry. Place turkey on a rotisserie and secure. Rub canola oil on turkey and season with salt, pepper, and paprika. Place rotisserie on grill. Cook turkey until it reaches an internal temperature of 170°F (about 1 1/2 hours). Be sure to measure at the thickest part of the meat, without touching bone or metal. Remove turkey from grill and let it rest for 20 minutes. Carve and serve.

Exchanges/Choices
6 Lean Meat

Basic Nutritional Values
Calories 235
   Calories from Fat 35
Total Fat 4 g
   Saturated Fat 0.6 g
   Trans Fat 0 g
Cholesterol 130 mg
Sodium 465 mg
Total Carbohydrate 0 g
   Dietary Fiber 0 g
   Sugars 0 g
Protein 47 g

Tips for the Kitchen

Because most grills are not large enough to handle a full turkey, I usually just use turkey breast. On average, it takes 15 minutes per pound to fully cook turkey, but always check the temperature first.

TOURNEDOS OF BEEF WITH SAUTÉED MUSHROOMS

SERVES 4
SERVING SIZE: 1/4 RECIPE

1	LB BEEF TENDERLOIN
3	TBSP OLIVE OIL
1	TBSP LEMON JUICE
1	TSP SALT
	PEPPER, TO TASTE
2	TBSP SHALLOTS, SMALL DICE
8	OZ WHITE BUTTON MUSHROOMS, WASHED AND QUARTERED
1	TBSP MINCED FRESH CHIVES

Exchanges/Choices
3 Lean Meat
2 1/2 Fat

Basic Nutritional Values
Calories 245
  Calories from Fat 145
Total Fat 16 g
  Saturated Fat 3.6 g
  Trans Fat 0 g
Cholesterol 60 mg
Sodium 630 mg
Total Carbohydrate 3 g
  Dietary Fiber 1 g
  Sugars 1 g
Protein 23 g

1. Cut beef tenderloin into 2-oz slices (eight equal pieces). Combine beef with 2 Tbsp olive oil, lemon juice, salt, pepper, and shallots; cover and refrigerate overnight. Place beef on a hot grill, and cook until desired doneness (145°F for medium and 160°F for well done).

2. Preheat a sauté pan and add 1 Tbsp olive oil. Add button mushrooms and sauté, tossing often, until golden brown. Add chives and toss to combine with mushrooms. Pour mushroom mixture over beef tournedos and serve.

Tips for the Kitchen

Tournedos of beef are thin, round slices of tenderloin.

GLAZED ORANGE CHICKEN

1 TBSP POULTRY SEASONING

4 CLOVES GARLIC, MINCED

1 SPRIG ROSEMARY

1 TBSP LEMON PEPPER

1 TSP RED PEPPER FLAKES

2 TBSP OLIVE OIL

4 SKINLESS, BONELESS CHICKEN BREASTS
   (ABOUT 1 LB TOTAL)

2 TBSP ORANGE MARMALADE

SERVES 4
SERVING SIZE: 1 BREAST

1. In a medium container, combine poultry seasoning, garlic, rosemary, lemon pepper, pepper flakes, and olive oil. Add chicken breasts and marinate for at least 2 hours.

2. Preheat a sauté pan and sear both sides of the chicken breasts to a golden brown. Place on a sheet pan and bake in a preheated 375°F oven to an internal temperature of 160°F.

3. Brush breasts with orange marmalade and serve.

Exchanges/Choices
1/2 Carbohydrate
3 Lean Meat
1 Fat

Basic Nutritional Values
Calories 225
  Calories from Fat 90
Total Fat 10 g
  Saturated Fat 1.7 g
  Trans Fat 0 g
Cholesterol 65 mg
Sodium 335 mg
Total Carbohydrate 10 g
  Dietary Fiber 1 g
  Sugars 7 g
Protein 25 g

PORK LOIN
STUFFED WITH SHRIMP

SERVES 16
SERVING SIZE: 1/16 RECIPE

4	LB BONELESS PORK LOIN, TRIMMED
2	TBSP OLIVE OIL
1	LB SHRIMP, COARSELY CHOPPED
1/2	LB ONIONS, SLICED
2	TBSP OLD BAY SEASONING
2	LB DRIED BREAD CRUMBS
1	BUNCH FRESH PARSLEY, CHOPPED
2	CUPS HOT CHICKEN STOCK (SEE RECIPE ON P. 24)
3/4	CUP EGG SUBSTITUTE
1	TSP SALT
1	TSP PEPPER

1. Place pork loin on a large cutting board and, using a sharp knife, horizontally slice the loin 1/2 inch above the cutting board. Begin to roll cut the loin of pork. As you cut, unroll the roast, similar to unrolling a roll of paper towels; continue cutting pork until one even layer of pork is completed. (You can also have the butcher do this at the store.) Place plastic wrap over the pork slices and, using a meat tenderizer, pound slices until they are about 1/4 inch to 1/2 inch thick. Set aside in the refrigerator.

2. In a large stockpot, add 1 Tbsp olive oil and sauté shrimp. When the shrimp is nearly done, add the onions and sweat until they are cooking but not browning. Add Old Bay and continue to cook. When onions are soft, remove from heat; add bread crumbs and parsley. Then, in a slow stream, add the chicken stock. Add the egg substitute and combine; mixture should be soft but tight. Allow to cool.

3. Place pork on a cutting board. Spread stuffing over 3/4 of the pork, leaving about 2 inches free on the end. Begin to roll the roast using the stuffing side first, rolling tightly until the last 2 inches, and continue to roll tightly.

4. Using butcher's twine, tie pork closed evenly, starting in the middle and working your way to the ends. Season roast with 1 Tbsp olive oil, salt, and pepper, and bake at 400°F for 15 minutes. Lower the oven to 250°F and bake to an internal temperature of 180°F. Remove from oven and allow to rest for 10 minutes. Carve to order, and remove the butcher's twine as you cut your servings.

Exchanges/Choices

3 Starch
4 Lean Meat
1/2 Fat

Basic Nutritional Values

Calories 430
  Calories from Fat 110
Total Fat 12 g
  Saturated Fat 3.5 g
  Trans Fat 0 g
Cholesterol 100 mg
Sodium 930 mg
Total Carbohydrate 43 g
  Dietary Fiber 3 g
  Sugars 4 g
Protein 34 g

This recipe is
high in sodium.

Tips for the Kitchen

This recipe is even better when served with the bourbon cranberry sauce (see recipe on p. 23).

Easy Mashed Potatoes

3	QUARTS WATER
1	LB YUKON GOLD POTATOES
3/4	CUP 1% LOW-FAT MILK
1	TBSP BUTTER
	PINCH WHITE PEPPER
1	TSP SALT

SERVES 6
SERVING SIZE: 1/2 CUP

Exchanges/Choices
1 Starch
1/2 Fat

Basic Nutritional Values
Calories 105
  Calories from Fat 20
Total Fat 2.5 g
  Saturated Fat 1.4 g
  Trans Fat 0 g
Cholesterol 5 mg
Sodium 425 mg
Total Carbohydrate 19 g
  Dietary Fiber 2 g
  Sugars 3 g
Protein 3 g

1. In a medium pot, bring water to a boil. Add the potatoes and simmer until they are tender. Drain well.

2. Add the remaining ingredients; blend thoroughly using a hand mixer. Serve hot.

Tips for the Kitchen

If Yukon Gold potatoes are not available, you can use Red Bliss potatoes instead with the skin on or off.

WILD RICE WITH DRIED CRANBERRIES

1 TBSP OLIVE OIL

1/2 CUP ONIONS, SMALL DICE

1 CUP WILD RICE

3 CUPS HOT CHICKEN STOCK (SEE RECIPE ON P. 24)

1 TSP WHITE PEPPER

1 CUP DRIED CRANBERRIES

SERVES 4
SERVING SIZE: 1/4 RECIPE

In a medium pot, heat the olive oil. Add onions and sweat them until translucent. Add wild rice; continue stirring. Add chicken stock and white pepper; bring to a simmer. Reduce heat to low and cover. Continue cooking for 25 minutes. Be sure to check that rice does not burn. When most of the liquid has been absorbed, add cranberries and stir to incorporate. Serve immediately.

Exchanges/Choices
1 1/2 Starch
1 1/2 Fruit
1/2 Fat

Basic Nutritional Values
Calories 240
  Calories from Fat 40
Total Fat 4.5 g
  Saturated Fat 0.6 g
  Trans Fat 0 g
Cholesterol 0 mg
Sodium 15 mg
Total Carbohydrate 49 g
  Dietary Fiber 4 g
  Sugars 22 g
Protein 5 g

PARMESAN ASPARAGUS

SERVES 4
SERVING SIZE: 1/4 RECIPE

1	LB FRESH ASPARAGUS
1	QUART WATER
1/2	TSP SALT
2	TSP EXTRA-VIRGIN OLIVE OIL
2	TBSP MINCED SHALLOTS
1/4	CUP FRESHLY GRATED PARMESAN CHEESE

Exchanges/Choices
1 Vegetable
1 Fat

Basic Nutritional Values
Calories 70
  Calories from Fat 40
Total Fat 4.5 g
  Saturated Fat 1.3 g
  Trans Fat 0 g
Cholesterol 5 mg
Sodium 115 mg
Total Carbohydrate 5 g
  Dietary Fiber 1 g
  Sugars 2 g
Protein 5 g

1. Wash the asparagus and pat dry. Remove about 1 inch from the bottom of each stalk.

2. In a medium pot, bring the water and salt to a simmer. Add the asparagus and cook until just tender, about 1–2 minutes. Remove asparagus and place on a serving dish.

3. In a small sauté pan, heat oil and add shallots. Sauté shallots until slightly browned. Pour shallot mixture over asparagus and sprinkle with cheese. Serve warm.

Braised Brussels Sprouts with Fresh Herbs and Fortified Chicken Stock

3/4 LB FRESH BRUSSELS SPROUTS

1 CUP FORTIFIED CHICKEN STOCK (SEE RECIPE ON P. 24)

1 TSP MINCED THYME

1 TSP MINCED OREGANO

1 TBSP MINCED CHIVES

SERVES 4
SERVING SIZE: 1/4 RECIPE

1. Wash the Brussels sprouts and pat them dry. Remove 1/8 inch of the stems and discard. Using a paring knife, cut an X into the stem of each sprout. Set aside.

2. In a medium sauté pan, bring the chicken stock to a simmer over high heat. Add the Brussels sprouts and cover. Lower the heat to medium; cook the sprouts until tender, about 15 minutes.

3. Remove the Brussels sprouts and keep them warm. Continue to simmer the chicken stock until the liquid is reduced to a syrupy consistency.

4. Return the Brussels sprouts and herbs to the chicken stock reduction and toss, coating lightly. Serve immediately.

Exchanges/Choices
2 Vegetable

Basic Nutritional Values
Calories 40
  Calories from Fat 5
Total Fat 0.5 g
  Saturated Fat 0.1 g
  Trans Fat 0 g
Cholesterol 5 mg
Sodium 25 mg
Total Carbohydrate 8 g
  Dietary Fiber 2 g
  Sugars 3 g
Protein 3 g

PERSIMMON PUDDING

SERVES 4
SERVING SIZE: 1/4 RECIPE

1   BOX SUGAR-FREE VANILLA PUDDING

1   PERSIMMON, PEELED AND PUREED

1   OZ LIGHT WHIPPED TOPPING

1   TSP CRUSHED PECANS

Exchanges/Choices
1 Carbohydrate

Basic Nutritional Values
Calories 55
  Calories from Fat 15
Total Fat 1.5 g
  Saturated Fat 0.8 g
  Trans Fat 0 g
Cholesterol 0 mg
Sodium 300 mg
Total Carbohydrate 11 g
  Dietary Fiber 0 g
  Sugars 3 g
Protein 0 g

1. Combine vanilla pudding and pureed persimmon until smooth.

2. Divide mixture evenly among four tall wineglasses, add a dollop of whipped topping, and finish with a sprinkle of crushed pecans.

Tips for the Kitchen

Persimmons are light yellow-orange to dark red-orange. They are available in the fruit section of most grocery stores. They are normally available in the fall, but can be found in other seasons.

PUMPKIN BITES

6	OZ WHIPPED CREAM CHEESE
1/4	CUP SUGAR
15	OZ PUMPKIN PUREE
1	TSP VANILLA
1/2	TSP CINNAMON
1/4	TSP GROUND GINGER
24	MINIATURE PHYLLO DOUGH SHELLS
1	CUP FAT-FREE WHIPPED TOPPING

SERVES 24
SERVING SIZE: 1 PUMPKIN BITE

Combine cream cheese, sugar, pumpkin puree, vanilla, cinnamon, and ground ginger until fully incorporated. Place mixture into a pastry bag with a star tip and portion into individual phyllo dough shells. Garnish with a small dollop of whipped topping. Serve immediately.

Exchanges/Choices
1/2 Carbohydrate
1/2 Fat

Basic Nutritional Values
Calories 55
  Calories from Fat 25
Total Fat 3 g
  Saturated Fat 1.2 g
  Trans Fat 0 g
Cholesterol 5 mg
Sodium 45 mg
Total Carbohydrate 6 g
  Dietary Fiber 0 g
  Sugars 3 g
Protein 0 g

APRICOTS AND CHOCOLATE

1   12-OZ BAG SEMISWEET CHOCOLATE CHIPS

24   PIECES DRIED APRICOTS

SERVES 24

SERVING SIZE: 1 APRICOT

1. In a double boiler, melt chocolate until smooth. Dip dried apricots into the chocolate, covering 3/4 of each apricot. You will have some leftover chocolate.

2. Place on a cooling rack and allow chocolate to harden. Place on serving dish and serve after dinner.

Exchanges/Choices
1/2 Carbohydrate

Basic Nutritional Values
Calories 30
  Calories from Fat 10
Total Fat 1 g
  Saturated Fat 0.7 g
  Trans Fat 0 g
Cholesterol 0 mg
Sodium 0 mg
Total Carbohydrate 5 g
  Dietary Fiber 0 g
  Sugars 4 g
Protein 0 g

Tips for the Kitchen

This is one of my favorite things during the holidays! You can add crushed nuts to make this dish crunchy.

INDEX

RECIPES BY NAME

RECIPES BY SUBJECT

Turkey (*see* Poultry)

Vegetables

Vinaigrettes

RECIPES BY CATEGORY

Essentials

Breakfast

Other Titles Available from the American Diabetes Association

American Diabetes Association Complete Guide to Diabetes, 4th Edition
by American Diabetes Association
Have all the tips and information on diabetes that you need close at hand. The world's largest collection of diabetes self-care tips, techniques, and tricks for solving diabetes-related problems is back in its fourth edition, and it's bigger and better than ever before.
Order no. 4809-04; **NEW LOW PRICE!** $19.95

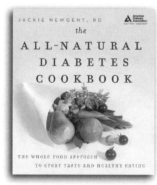

Diabetes Meal Planning Made Easy, 3rd Edition
by Hope S. Warshaw, MMSc, RD, CDE, BC-ADM
Let expert Hope Warshaw show you how to change unhealthy eating habits while continuing to enjoy the foods you love! This book serves up techniques for changing your eating habits over time so that changes you make are the ones that last for life!
Order no. 4706-03; Price $14.95

The All-Natural Diabetes Cookbook: The Whole Food Approach to Great Taste and Healthy Eating
by Jackie Newgent, RD
Instead of relying on artificial sweeteners or not-so-real substitutions to reduce calories, sugar, and fat, *The All-Natural Diabetes Cookbook* takes a different approach, focusing on naturally delicious fresh foods and whole-food ingredients to create fantastic meals that deliver amazing taste and well-rounded nutrition. And absolutely nothing is artificial.
Order no. 4663-01; Price $18.95

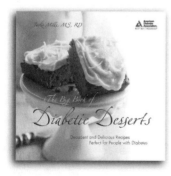

The Big Book of Diabetic Desserts
by Jackie Mills, MS, RD
This first-ever collection of guilty pleasures proves that people with diabetes never have to say no to dessert again. Packed with familiar favorites and some delicious new surprises, *The Big Book of Diabetic Desserts* has more than 150 tantalizing treats that will satisfy any sweet tooth.
Order no. 4664-01; Price $18.95

To order these and other great American Diabetes Association titles, call 1-800-232-6733 or visit http://store.diabetes.org.
American Diabetes Association titles are available in bookstores nationwide.